THE HADITH

THE SUNNA OF MOHAMMED

BILL WARNER, PHD

CENTER FOR THE STUDY OF
POLITICAL ISLAM

THE HADITH

THE SUNNA OF MOHAMMED

BILL WARNER, PHD

CENTER FOR THE STUDY OF
POLITICAL ISLAM

ISBN13 978-1-936659-01-2

V 09.14.2016

PUBLISHED BY CSPI, LLC
WWW.CSPIPUBLISHING.COM

PRINTED IN THE USA

TABLE OF CONTENTS

This book is dedicated to the
millions of victims of jihad over the past 1400 years.
May you read this and become a voice for the voiceless.

PREFACE

The Center for the Study of Political Islam, CSPI, teaching method is the easiest and quickest way to learn about Islam.

Authoritative

There are only two ultimate authorities about Islam—Allah and Mohammed. All of the curriculum in the CSPI method is from the Koran and the Sunna (the words and deeds of Mohammed). The knowledge you get in CSPI is powerful, authoritative and irrefutable. You learn the facts about the ideology of Islam from its ultimate sources.

Story-telling

Facts are hard to remember, stories are easy to remember. The most important story in Islam is the life of Mohammed. Once you know the story of Mohammed, all of Islam is easy to understand.

Systemic Knowledge

The easiest way to study Islam is to first see the whole picture. The perfect example of this is the Koran. The Koran alone cannot be understood, but when the life of Mohammed is added, the Koran is straight forward.

There is no way to understand Islam one idea at the time, because there is no context. Context, like story-telling, makes the facts and ideas simple to understand. The best analogy is that when the jig saw puzzle is assembled, the image on the puzzle is easy to see. But looking at the various pieces, it is difficult to see the picture.

Levels of Learning

The ideas of Islam are very foreign to our civilization. It takes repetition to grasp the new ideas. The CSPI method uses four levels of training to teach the doctrine in depth. The first level is designed for a beginner. Each level repeats the basics for in depth learning.

When you finish the first level you will have seen the entire scope of Islam, The in depth knowledge will come from the next levels.

Political Islam, Not Religious Islam

Islam has a political doctrine and a religious doctrine. Its political doctrine is of concern for everyone, while religious Islam is of concern only for Muslims.

Books Designed for Learning

Each CSPI book fits into a teaching system. Most of the paragraphs have an index number which means that you can confirm for yourself how factual the books are by verifying from the original source texts.

LEVEL 1

INTRODUCTION TO THE TRILOGY AND SHARIA

The Life of Mohammed, The Hadith, Lectures on the Foundations of Islam, The Two Hour Koran, Sharia Law for Non-Muslims, Self Study on Political Islam, Level 1

LEVEL 2

APPLIED DOCTRINE, SPECIAL TOPICS

The Doctrine of Women, The Doctrine of Christians and Jews, The Doctrine of Slavery, Self-Study on Political Islam, Level 2, Psychology of the Muslim, Factual Persuasion

LEVEL 3

INTERMEDIATE TRILOGY AND SHARIA

Mohammed and the Unbelievers, Political Traditions of Mohammed, Simple Koran, Self-Study of Political Islam, Level 3, Sources of the Koran, selected topics from *Reliance of the Traveller*

LEVEL 4

ORIGINAL SOURCE TEXTS

The Life of Muhammed, Guillaume; any *Koran, Sahih Bukhari,* selected topics, *Mohammed and Charlemagne Revisited,* Scott.

With the completion of Level 4 you are prepared to read both popular and academic texts.

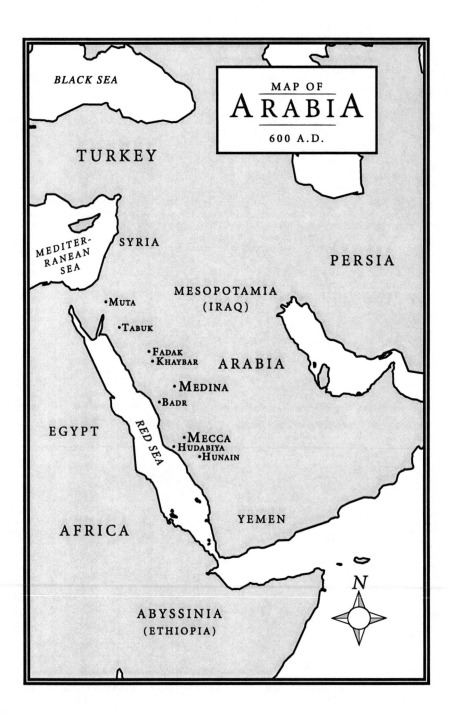

OVERVIEW

CHAPTER 1

One of the easiest ways to study Islam is to learn about Mohammed through his Traditions, called the Hadith.

THE ISLAMIC BIBLE—THE TRILOGY

Islam is defined by the words of Allah in the Koran, and the words and actions of Mohammed, the *Sunna.*

The Sunna is found in two collections of texts—the Sira (Mohammed's life) and the Hadith. The Koran says 91 times that Mohammed's words and actions are considered to be the perfect pattern for humanity.

A hadith, or tradition, is a brief story about what Mohammed did or said. A collection of hadiths is called a Hadith. There are many collections of hadiths, but the most authoritative are those by Bukhari and Abu Muslim, the ones used in this book.

So the Trilogy is the Koran, the Sira and the Hadith. Most people think that the Koran is the "bible" of Islam, but it is only about 14% of the total textual doctrine. The Trilogy is the foundation and totality of Islam.

FIGURE 1.1: THE RELATIVE SIZES OF THE TRILOGY TEXTS

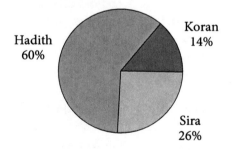

Islam is defined by the words of Allah in the Koran, and the words and actions of Mohammed, the *Sunna.*

No one text of the Trilogy can stand by itself; it is impossible to understand any one of the texts without the other supporting texts. The Koran, Sira, and Hadith are a seamless whole and speak with one voice. If it is in the Trilogy it is Islam.

FIGURE 1.2: THUS SUNNA OF MOHAMMED

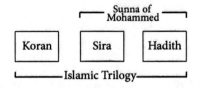

INTRODUCTION TO THE HADITH

A hadith, or tradition, usually only a paragraph long, is an action, brief story, or conversation about or by Mohammed. The action can be as elementary as Mohammed's drinking a glass of water or putting on his sandals. A collection of these stories is called the Hadith or Traditions. So the Hadith is a collection of hadiths (the actual plural of hadith is *ahadith*).

The Hadith contains the *Sunna* (the ideal speech or action) of Mohammed, that is, his pronouncements. The actual words or deeds, then, that one should follow, are the Sunna; the story that gives us the Sunna is the hadith.

There are many collectors of hadiths, but the two most authoritative collectors were Bukhari (Muhammad Ibn Ismail Al-Bukhari) and Muslim (Abu Al-Husayn Muslim). Most of the hadiths in this book come from Bukhari. From 600,000 hadiths, he took the most reliable, about 7000, and recorded them in *Sahih Bukhari*. Muslim's work is called *Sahih Muslim*. Sahih means "authentic".

Bukhari's Hadith has about 7000 hadiths. It is vast, but the large number of hadiths is an illusion. If you were to go through the collection and combine all of the hadiths that describe the same scene, there are probably fewer than a thousand hadiths that are unique.

WHAT IS THIS BOOK?

Selections have been made from over thirteen thousand hadiths from Bukhari and Muslim and have been sorted into categories. Most of these hadiths concern political Islam, in other words, how Islam treats non-Muslims.

These hadiths are foundational literature. The Koran repeatedly tells all Muslims to copy the perfect pattern of Mohammed's actions and words. For Islam, Mohammed is the model political leader, husband, warrior, philosopher, religious leader, and neighbor. Mohammed is the ideal pattern of man for all times and all places.

KAFIR

The word Kafir will be used in this book instead of "unbeliever", the standard word. Unbeliever is a neutral term. The Koran defines the Kafir and Kafir is not a neutral word. A Kafir is not merely someone who does not agree with Islam, but a Kafir is evil, disgusting, the lowest form of life. Kafirs can be tortured, killed, lied to and cheated. So the usual word "unbeliever" does not reflect the political reality of Islam.

The Koran says that the Kafir may be deceived, plotted against, hated, enslaved, mocked, tortured and worse. The word is usually translated as "unbeliever" but this translation is wrong. The word "unbeliever" is logically and emotionally neutral, whereas, Kafir is the most abusive, prejudiced and hateful word in any language.

There are many religious names for Kafirs: polytheists, idolaters, People of the Book (Christians and Jews), Buddhists, atheists, agnostics, and pagans. Kafir covers them all, because no matter what the religious name is, they can all be treated the same. What Mohammed said and did to polytheists can be done to any other category of Kafir.

Islam devotes a great amount of energy to the Kafir. The majority (64%) of the Koran is devoted to the Kafir, and nearly all of the Sira (81%) deals with Mohammed's struggle with them. The Hadith (Traditions) devotes 37% of the text to Kafirs[1.]. Overall, the Trilogy devotes 51% of its content to the Kafir.

FIGURE 1.3: THE AMOUNT OF TEXT DEVOTED OF KAFIR

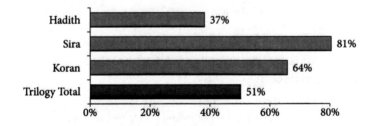

Here are a few of the Koran references:

A Kafir can be beheaded—

> 47:4 *When you encounter the Kafirs on the battlefield, cut off their heads until you have thoroughly defeated them and then take the prisoners and tie them up firmly.*

---

1   http://cspipublishing.com/statistical/TrilogyStats/AmtTxtDevotedKafir.html

A Kafir can be plotted against—

86:15 *They plot and scheme against you [Mohammed], and I plot and scheme against them. Therefore, deal calmly with the Kafirs and leave them alone for a while.*

A Kafir can be terrorized—

8:12 *Then your Lord spoke to His angels and said, "I will be with you. Give strength to the believers. I will send terror into the Kafirs' hearts, cut off their heads and even the tips of their fingers!"*

A Muslim is not the friend of a Kafir—

3:28 *Believers should not take Kafirs as friends in preference to other believers. Those who do this will have none of Allah's protection and will only have themselves as guards. Allah warns you to fear Him for all will return to Him.*

A Kafir is cursed—

33:61 *They [Kafirs] will be cursed, and wherever they are found, they will be seized and murdered. It was Allah's same practice with those who came before them, and you will find no change in Allah's ways.*

KAFIRS AND PEOPLE OF THE BOOK

Muslims tell Christians and Jews that they are special. They are "People of the Book" and are brothers in the Abrahamic faith. But in Islam you are a Christian, if and only if, you believe that Christ was a man who was a prophet of Allah; there is no Trinity; Jesus was not crucified nor resurrected and that He will return to establish Sharia law. Nothing in Christian doctrine agrees with the Islamic definition of what a Christian is.

Under Islam, to be a true Jew you must believe that the Torah is corrupt and Mohammed is the last in the line of Jewish prophets.

This verse can be seen as positive:

Koran 5:77 *Say: Oh, People of the Book, do not step out of the bounds of truth in your religion, and do not follow the desires of those who have gone wrong and led many astray. They have themselves gone astray from the even way.*

Islamic doctrine is dualistic, so there is an opposite view as well. Here is the last verse written about the People of the Book. [You cannot understand the Koran without knowing the principle of *abrogation*. The Koran has many contradictory verses. Abrogation says that the later verse is stronger or better than an earlier verse.] Since chapter 9 is the final chapter of the Koran, the last one written, it is the final word. It is stronger than all of the "peaceful" verses that precede it. It calls for Muslims to make war on the People of the Book who do not believe in the religion of truth, Islam.

> Koran 9:29 *Make war on those who have received the Scriptures [Jews and Christians] but do not believe in Allah or in the Last Day. They do not forbid what Allah and His Messenger have forbidden. The Christians and Jews do not follow the religion of truth until they submit and pay the poll tax [jizya] and they are humiliated.*

The sentence "They do not forbid..." means that they do not accept Sharia law; "until they submit" means submission to Sharia law.

In Islam, Christians and Jews are called infidels and "People of the Book"; Hindus are polytheists and pagans. The terms infidel, People of the Book, pagan and polytheist are religious words. Only the word "Kafir" shows the common political treatment of the Christian, Jew, Hindu, Buddhist, animist, atheist and humanist. What is done to a pagan can be done to a Christian, Jew or any other Kafir.

It is simple. If you don't believe that Mohammed is the prophet of Allah, then you are a Kafir.

The word Kafir will be used in this book instead of "unbeliever", "non-Muslim" or "disbeliever". Unbeliever or non-Muslim are neutral terms, but Kafir is not a neutral word. It is extremely bigoted and biased.

THE THREE VIEWS OF ISLAM

There are three points of view in dealing with Islam. The point of view depends upon how you feel about Mohammed. If you believe Mohammed is the prophet of Allah, then you are a believer. If you don't, you are a *Kafir*. The third viewpoint is that of a Kafir who is an apologist for Islam.

Apologists do not believe that Mohammed was a prophet, but they never say anything that would displease a Muslim. Apologists never offend Islam and condemn any analysis that is critical of Islam as being biased.

Let us give an example of the three points of view.

In Medina, Mohammed sat all day long beside his 12-year-old wife while they watched as the heads of 800 Jews were removed by the sword.[2] Their heads were cut off because they had said that Mohammed was not the prophet of Allah. Muslims view these deaths as necessary because denying Mohammed's prophet-hood was an offense against Islam and beheading is the accepted method of punishment, sanctioned by Allah.

---

2   *The Life of Muhammad*, A. Guillaume, Oxford University Press, 1982, pg. 464.

Kafirs look at this event as proof of the jihadic violence of Islam and as an evil act. They call it ethnic cleansing.

Apologists say that this was a historic event, that all cultures have violence in their past, and that no judgment should be passed. They ignore the Islamic belief that the Sunna, Mohammed's words and deeds in the past, is the perfect model for today and tomorrow and forever. They ignore the fact that this past event of the beheading of 800 Jewish men continues to be acceptable in the present and the future, thus the fate of Daniel Pearl (a reporter who was beheaded on camera).

According to the different points of view, killing the 800 Jews was either evil, a perfect godly act or only another historical event, take your pick.

This book is written from the Kafir point of view and is therefore, Kafir-centric. Everything in this book views Islam from how it affects Kafirs, non-Muslims. This also means that the religion is of little importance. Only a Muslim cares about the religion of Islam, but all Kafirs are affected by Islam's political views.

Notice that there is no right and wrong here, merely different points of view that cannot be reconciled. There is no possible resolution between the view of the Kafir and the Muslim. The apologist tries to bring about a bridge building compromise, but it is not logically possible.

MAXIM

Islam is primarily a political ideology. No action or statement by Islam can be understood without understanding its origins in the Trilogy. Any analysis, statement, or opinion about Islam is incomplete without a reference to the Trilogy. The Trilogy is the source and basis of all Islamic politics, diplomacy, history, philosophy, religion, and culture.

THE REFERENCE SYSTEM

References within this work:

2:123 is a reference to the Koran, chapter 2, verse 123.

B1,3,4 is a reference to *Sahih Bukhari*, volume 1, book 3, number 4.

M012, 1234 is a reference to *Sahih Muslim*, book 12, number 1234.

This book is adapted from *The Political Traditions of Mohammed* by CSPI Publishing.

ETHICS

*9:63 Do they not know that whoever opposes Allah
and His Messenger will abide in the fire of Hell, where
they will remain forever? This is the great shame.*

Outsiders judge a religion by its ethics. They are not concerned with what it teaches about salvation or life after death, but they care greatly what the religion tells members about outsiders. The foundation of this interaction between adherents and non-members is ethics.

BROTHERHOOD

The brother of a Muslim is another Muslim.

B1,2,12 Mohammed: "True faith comes when a man's personal desires mirror his wishes for other Muslims."

B9,85,83 Mohammed: "A Muslim is a brother to other Muslims. He should never oppress them nor should he facilitate their oppression. Allah will satisfy the needs of those who satisfy the needs of their brothers."

TRUTH

In Islam something that is not true is not always a lie.

B3,49,857 Mohammed: "A man who brings peace to the people by making up good words or by saying nice things, though untrue, does not lie."

An oath by a Muslim is flexible.

B8,78,618 Abu Bakr faithfully kept his oaths until Allah revealed to Mohammed the atonement for breaking them. Afterwards he said, "If I make a pledge and later discover a more worthy pledge, then I will take the better action and make amends for my earlier promise."

When deception advances Islam, the deception is not a sin.

B5,59,369 Mohammed asked, "Who will kill Ka'b, the enemy of Allah and Mohammed?"

Bin Maslama rose and responded, "O Mohammed! Would it please you if I killed him?"

Mohammed answered, "Yes."

7

Bin Maslama then said, "Give me permission to deceive him with lies so that my plot will succeed."

Mohammed replied, "You may speak falsely to him."

Ali was raised by Mohammed from the age of ten and became the fourth caliph. Ali pronounced the following on lies and deception.

B9,84,64 When I relate to you the words of Mohammed, by Allah, I would rather die than bear false witness to his teachings. However, if I should say something unrelated to the prophet, then it might very well be a lie so that I might deceive my enemy.

Deceit in war:

M032,6303 According to Mohammed, someone who strives to promote harmony amongst the faithful and says or conveys good things is not a liar. Ibn Shihab said that he had heard only three exceptions to the rules governing false statements: lies are permissible in war, to reconcile differences between the faithful, and to reconcile a husband and wife through the manipulation or twisting of words.

The name for deception that advances Islam is taqiyya (safeguard, conceal-ment, piety). But a Muslim must never lie to another Muslim. A lie should never be told unless there is no other way to accomplish the task Al Tabarani, in Al Awsat, said, "Lies are sins except when they are told for the welfare of a Muslim or for saving him from a disaster." 1

LAW

The hadiths are the basis of the Sharia, Islamic law. Here is a hadith about capital crimes. Killing a Kafir is not a capital crime.

B1,3,111 I [Abu] asked Ali, "Do you know of any sources of law that were revealed to Mohammed other than the Koran?" Ali responded, "None except for Allah's law, or the ability of reason given by Allah to a Muslim, or these written precepts I possess." I said, "What are these written rules?" Ali answered, "They concern the blood money paid by a killer to a victim's relatives, the method of ransoming a captive's release from the enemy, and the law that a Muslim must never be killed as punishment for killing a Kafir."

---

1.   Bat Ye'or, *The Dhimmi* (Cranbury, N.J.: Associated University Presses, 2003), 392.

TREATMENT OF FELLOW MUSLIMS

Weapons in the mosque are acceptable. The mosque is a political center as well as a community center and a place of worship.

B1,8,443 Mohammed: "Arrows should be held by their heads when carried through mosques or markets so that they do not harm a Muslim."

B8,73,70 Mohammed: "Harming a Muslim is an evil act; killing a Muslim means rejecting Allah."

POSITION TOWARD OTHER RELIGIONS

Mohammed's deathbed wishes were to create religious apartheid in Arabia and to use money to influence Kafirs for Islam.

B4,52,288 [...] "On his deathbed Mohammed gave three final orders saying, 'First, drive the Kafirs from Arabia. Second, give gifts and show respect to foreign officials as I have done.' I forgot the third command."

SLAVERY

It is forbidden to capture a Muslim and make him a slave. If a slave converts to Islam, then there is a benefit in freeing him. But there is no benefit in freeing a Kafir slave. Islamic slavery is a blessing because sooner or later the slave or the slave's descendants will convert to Islam in order to be free.

B3,46,693 Mohammed said, "If a man frees a Muslim slave, Allah will free him from the fires of Hell in the same way that he freed the slave." Bin Marjana said that, after he related that revelation to Ali, the man freed a slave for whom he had been offered one thousand dinars by Abdullah.

ETHICS OF KILLING WOMEN AND CHILDREN IN JIHAD

Here are two examples that determine the rules of jihad. They contradict each other, so the resolution is that either can be used as needed.

M019,4319 In one of Mohammed's battles, it was discovered that a woman had been killed by the Muslims; however, he did not approve of killing women and children.

M019,4321 According to Sa'b B. Jaththama, Mohammed said, "They are from them," when told of the killing of women and children by Muslims during a raid.

This is the Sunna of Mohammed

JIHAD

CHAPTER 3

*61:11 Believe in Allah and His messenger and fight valiantly
for Allah's cause [jihad] with both your wealth and your
lives. It would be better for you, if you only knew it!*

The ethical system of the Hadith prepares the foundation of jihad. There is one set of ethics for the Muslim and another set of ethics for the Kafir. There are two ways to deal with Kafirs. One is to treat them as inferiors but in a kindly way. The other is jihad. About 21% of Bukhari is about jihad.

Jihad is a unique word. Its actual meaning is struggle or effort. Islam talks of two kinds—the lesser jihad and the greater jihad. The greater jihad is spiritual effort or internal struggle, to stop smoking, for example, or control one's greed. However, the term "lesser jihad" never occurs in any authoritative hadith. There are about 2% of the hadiths in Bukhari that hold up other things as equal to jihad. The other 98% of the jihad hadiths refer to armed violence. It was violence that gave Islam its success and that is why nearly every hadith calls the jihad the best action a Muslim can perform.

Jihad, armed struggle, is usually called "holy war," but this term is simplistic and far too narrow. It means, in fact, fighting in the cause of Allah, and it encompasses an entire way of life.

The dual ethics established by the sacred texts of Islam—treating Muslims one way and Kafirs another—are the basis of jihad. Perhaps the clearest expression of this duality is a phrase known to all Muslims: The world is divided into—

dar al Islam, land of submission, and
dar al harb, land of war.

The land of war is the country that is free of Islam, free of Allah. The land of the Kafir must become the land of those who have submitted and are the slaves of Allah. The Trilogy repeatedly stresses that Islam should be in a state of constant pressure against Kafirs; therefore, the relation between Islam and the rest of the world is sacred war or temporary peace. This struggle is eternal, universal, and obligatory for the

Muslim community. The only pause in jihad comes through the need for Islam to strengthen itself. Peace is temporary. War is permanent.

Jihad is laid out in all three of the Trilogy texts.

JIHAD IN THE HADITH

The Hadith spells out the details of jihad. Who can be killed, under what circumstances, at what times, the actual words to be said upon attack, how to handle defeat, what to do with prisoners, how to build morale, and more are drawn from the ideal words and actions of Mohammed. The Hadith is a precise tactical manual for jihad.

The hadiths call armed struggle "fighting in Allah's Cause" or "Allah's Cause." Many of the hadiths focus on jihad.

THE FUNDAMENTALS OF JIHAD

This hadith summarizes all the key elements of jihad. (Only the fourth item, the Day of Resurrection, is purely religious in nature). It tells us that the whole world must submit to Islam; Kafirs are the enemy simply by not being Muslims. To achieve this dominance Islam may use terror and violence. It may use psychological warfare, fear, theft. It may take the spoils of war from Kafirs. Violence and terror are made sacred by the Koran. Peace comes only with submission to Islam.

B1,7,331 Mohammed:

I have been given five things which were not given to any one else before me:

1. Allah made me *victorious by awe, by His frightening my enemies* for a distance of one month's journey.

2. *The earth has been made for me and for my followers,* a place for praying and a place to perform rituals; therefore, anyone of my followers can pray wherever the time of a prayer is due.

3. *The spoils of war has been made lawful for me* yet it was not lawful for anyone else before me.

4. I have been given the right of intercession on the Day of Resurrection.

5. Every Prophet used to be sent to his nation only but *I have been sent to all mankind.* [Emphasis added.]

Political Islam is universal and eternal.

M001,0031 Mohammed: "I have been ordered to wage war against mankind until they accept that there is no god but Allah and that they believe I am His prophet and accept all revelations spoken through me. When they do these things I will protect their lives and property unless otherwise justified by Islamic law, in which case their fate lies in Allah's hands."

OBLIGATION

Jihad is one of the best actions that a Muslim can perform.

B2,26,594 Someone asked Mohammed, "What is the greatest act a Muslim can perform?" He said, "Accept Allah as the only god and that I am His prophet." Mohammed was then asked, "What is the next best act?" He answered, "To wage holy war in the name of Allah." Mohammed was then asked, "What is the next highest good?" He replied, "To make the sacred pilgrimage."

To be a real Muslim, one must aspire to be a jihadist.

M020,4696 Mohammed: "The man who dies without participating in jihad, who never desired to wage holy war, dies the death of a hypocrite."

Here we have prophetic hadiths. Jihad will be practiced into the future.

B4,152,146 Mohammed: "A time will come when the people will wage holy war, and it will be asked, 'Is there any amongst you who has enjoyed the company of Mohammed?' They will say: 'Yes.' And then victory will be bestowed upon them. They will wage holy war again, and it will be asked: 'Is there any among you who has enjoyed the company of the companions of Mohammed?' They will say: 'Yes.' And then victory will be bestowed on them."

M020,4712 Mohammed: "You shall conquer many lands and Allah will grant you victory over your enemies in battle, but none of you should stop practicing for war."

Fighting in jihad is demanded for all Muslims except for the frail or the crippled. To sit at home is inferior to jihad. Jihad is an obligation for all times and all places and for all Muslims.

B6,60,118 After the following verse was revealed to Mohammed, he called for a scribe,

> "Not equal are those believers who sit at home and those who strive and fight in the Cause of Allah."

After the scribe arrived with his writing utensils, Mohammed dictated his revelation. Ibn Um Maktum, who was present, exclaimed, "O Mohammed! But I am blind." A new revelation was then revealed that said:

4:95 *Believers who stay at home in safety, other than those who are disabled, are not equal to those who fight with their wealth and their lives for Allah's cause [jihad].*

When the leader calls for jihad, every Muslim should take part immediately.

B4,52,42 Mohammed: "After the conquest of Mecca, there is no need to migrate to Medina, but holy war and the willingness to participate still remain. If your ruler demands warriors, answer his call immediately."

Jihad is the best deed. The smallest action in jihad is rewarded more than prayer and fasting.

B4,52,44 A man said to Mohammed, "Tell me what act is rewarded as much as jihad." Mohammed replied, "I do not know of any." The prophet added, "Can a Muslim warrior, while in the field of battle, perform his prayers according to ritual or fast without stopping?" The man said, "No one can do that." Abu-Huraira then added, "The Muslim jihadi is rewarded by Allah merely for the footsteps of his mount while it is tethered and grazing."

An ordinary jihadist is superior to a saint.

B4,52,45 Someone asked, "Mohammed, who is the best person?" Mohammed said, "A Muslim who uses all of his strength and resources striving in Allah's cause." The person then asked, "Who is the next best person?" Mohammed replied, "A Muslim who remains secluded from the world, praying to Allah and not bothering the people with foolishness."

A jihadist fights so that Islam will triumph, not just for wealth or fame. The jihadist is the purest and best Muslim.

B4,52,65 A man asked Mohammed, "One man fights for wealth, one man fights to achieve fame, and another fights for pride. Who among them fights for the cause of Allah?" Mohammed said, "The man who fights so that Islam should dominate is the man who fights for Allah's cause."

All the Kafirs who fight against jihad are doomed to burn in Hell for defending their culture and civilization.

B4,52,72 Mohammed told us that Allah revealed to him that "any holy warrior killed will go to Paradise." Umar asked the prophet, "Is it true that Muslims killed in battle will go to Paradise and Kafirs who are killed in battle will go to Hell?" Mohammed said, "Yes."

A Muslim should support jihadists in every way. This includes financing the fighters and supporting their families.

B4,52,96 Mohammed: "Anyone who arms a jihadist is rewarded just as a fighter would be; anyone who gives proper care to a holy warrior's dependents is rewarded just as a fighter would be."

Practicing jihad for even one day puts a believer in Paradise and is better than all the world.

B4,52,142 Mohammed: "To battle Kafirs in jihad for even one day is greater than the entire earth and everything on it. A spot in Paradise smaller than your riding crop is greater than the entire earth and everything on it. A day or a night's travel in jihad is greater than the entire world and everything on it."

Jihad cannot stop until all of the world has submitted to Islam. All Kafirs' lives and wealth can and will be taken by jihad. Only those who submit to Islam will be spared.

B4,52,196 Mohammed: "I have been directed to fight the Kafir until every one of them admits, 'There is only one god and that is Allah.' Whoever says, 'There is only one god and that is Allah,' his body and possessions will be protected by me except for violations of Islamic law, in which case his fate is with Allah, to be punished or forgiven, as He sees fit."

INVESTMENT OF MONEY IN JIHAD

Allah rewards those who give to jihad and curses those who do not.

B2,24,522 Mohammed: "Two angels descend from Paradise each day. One says, 'O, Allah! Reward those who contribute to jihad,' and the other says, 'O, Allah! Kill those who refuse to support jihad.'"

Allah says a Muslim should spend his money on jihad.

B6,60,41 Hudhaifa said, "The following verse was revealed to Mohammed regarding the financial support of jihad."

> 2:195 *Spend your wealth generously for Allah's cause [jihad] and do not use your own hands to contribute to your destruction. Do good, for surely Allah loves those that do good.*

M020,4668 Mohammed: "A person who financially supports a fighter for jihad is morally equivalent to an actual fighter. A person who cares for a warrior's family during his service is morally equivalent to an actual fighter."

GOALS

The goal of jihad is the dominance of Islam over all other political systems and religions.

B1,3,125 A man asked Mohammed, "Mohammed, what manner of fighting can be considered done for the sake of Allah? Some fight because they are angry and some for their pride." Mohammed looked up at the man and said, "The man who fights to make Islam dominant is the man who fights for Allah's cause."

REWARDS

A Muslim martyr is one who kills for Allah and Islam. But his killing must be pure and devoted only to Allah. If his motivation is pure, then the jihadist will achieve Paradise or be able to take the wealth of the Kafir.

B1,2,35 Mohammed said, "The man who joins jihad, compelled by nothing except sincere belief in Allah and His Prophets, and survives, will be rewarded by Allah either in the afterlife or with the spoils of war. If he is killed in battle and dies a martyr, he will be admitted into Paradise. Were it not for the difficulties it would cause my followers, I would never stay behind while my soldiers head off for jihad. If I could, I would love to be martyred in jihad, be resurrected, and martyred again and again for Allah."

No matter what sins a jihadist commits, he will not go to Hell.

B2,13,30 I [Abu Abs] heard Mohammed say, "Anyone who even gets his feet dirty performing jihad will be saved from Hell by Allah."

The pure jihadist must commit his life and wealth to jihad. If he can reach this highest form of devotion, then not even the pilgrimage to Mecca (the Hajj) can surpass it.

B2,15,86 Mohammed said, "No good act during the rest of the year is better than departing on Hajj." Some of his companions asked, "What about jihad?" Mohammed answered, "Even jihad is inferior unless a man knowingly risks and loses both life and property for the sake of Allah."

M020,4649 Mohammed: "Except debt, all sins of a martyr are forgiven."

Paradise lies in the shade of swords.

M020,4681 Mohammed said, "Certainly, the gates of Paradise lie in the shade of swords." A shabby man rose and asked Abu Musa if he had heard Mohammed say this. "Yes," he replied. The shabby man then rejoined his friends and said his good-byes. He then unsheathed his sword, broke and discarded its scabbard, advanced upon the enemy, and fought until he was killed.

M020,4694 Mohammed: "A man who sincerely pursues martyrdom, even if he is not killed, shall still receive its reward."

A jihadist can benefit Islam and achieve personal gain.

B3,34,313 We departed with Mohammed in the year of the battle of Hunain. Mohammed gave me a captured suit of armor which I sold. I [Abu Qatada] took the money from the armor and bought a garden near the Bani Salama tribe. That was the first property I received after converting to Islam.

Mohammed often used money to influence others about Islam.

B4,53,374 Mohammed: "I give money to the Quraysh to tempt them into remaining true to Islam, because they are new to the faith and their lives of ignorance are a short distance away."

To die in jihad is the best life.

B5,59,377 During the battle of Uhud, a man asked Mohammed, "Where will I go if I am killed in battle?" Mohammed said, "Paradise." The man then threw away the meal that he was carrying, joined the battle, and fought until he was killed.

Jihad had to be waged far from Arabia and that meant fast transportation, so Mohammed used the rewards of jihad to build up his cavalry. He was a military genius who planned far ahead.

B5,59,537 The day Khaybar fell, Mohammed distributed the spoils by giving one share to the fighter and two shares to the owner of a horse. Nafi', a sub-narrator, elaborated, saying, "If a warrior supplied his own horse he received three shares; if he did not have a horse, he received only one."

No matter how little a Muslim does, if he dies in jihad, he will be given the highest rewards. Good works and morality pale in comparison to the rewards of jihad.

B4,52,63 A man, his face shielded by his helmet, asked Mohammed, "Should I join the battle or accept Islam first?" Mohammed answered, "Accept Allah and then join the fight." The man accepted Islam and was killed shortly after. Mohammed said, "A small effort but a great prize. Even though he did not do much after accepting Islam, he shall be richly rewarded."

Enslavement of the Kafirs and theft of their property were made sacred for Mohammed. Since Mohammed is the ideal pattern of behavior for all Muslims at all times and all places, the wealth of Kafirs is meant to be taken by others in Islam.

B4,53,351 Mohammed: "Allah has made it legal for me to take spoils of war."

Allah has a contractual agreement with all jihadists. If they die in jihad, Allah will reward them above all people. If they don't die, then they can profit by theft. So the jihadist has guarantees of profit in both this world and the next.

B4,53,352 Mohammed: "Allah promises the jihadi with pure intent either a place in Paradise or a return to his home with spoils of war and the guarantee of Allah's reward in the afterlife."

SEX

Forced sex with the female captives of jihad was standard practice for Mohammed and his companions. These captives became slaves used for sex, and Mohammed had his choice of the most attractive new slaves. This is the ideal pattern of Islam.

B3,34,431 One of the captives was a beautiful Jewess, Safiya. Dihya had her first, but she was given to Mohammed next.

Mohammed accepted the forced sex with Kafirs.

B3,34,432 While sitting with Mohammed, I [Abu Said Al-Khudri] asked, "Mohammed, sometimes we receive female slaves as our share of the spoils. Naturally, we are concerned about their retaining their value [the sex slaves were worth less money if they were pregnant when sold]. How do you feel about *coitus interruptus*?" Mohammed asked, "Do you do that? It is better not to do that. It is Allah's will whether or not a child is born."

Suicide is a sin in Islam, but killing oneself in jihad is not considered suicide; it is actually the highest form of Islam.

B9,83,29 Our company was traveling to Khaybar with Mohammed when someone called out, "Amir, sing some of your camel-driving songs." He complied, singing several songs whose rhythm mimicked the gait of camels. Mohammed was pleased and asked, "Who is that man?" "Amir," someone told him. Mohammed then said, "May Allah show mercy to him." Several of us said, "Mohammed, we hope that you will let him stay with us for a while," but he was killed early the next day.

We were very upset. Several people remarked, "It is too bad that all of Amir's good deeds have gone to waste, because he is damned for killing himself." When I heard those remarks, I went to Mohammed and said,

"Prophet of Allah, I would sacrifice my father for you, but the people say that Amir is damned." Mohammed said, "Then those people lie. Amir will be doubly rewarded because he strove to be obedient to Allah, and he fought in jihad. No other death would bring so great a reward."

In jihad, patience is a virtue.

B4,52,210 Once during battle, Mohammed spoke to the people as the sun was going down and said, "Do not willingly go into battle and beg Allah to protect you from harm. If you do go into battle, have patience and remember that Paradise lies in the shadow of swords." Mohammed then said, "Allah, bestower of the Koran, master of the elements, conqueror of the pagans, defeat the Kafir and give us victory."

Assassination is a tactic of jihad and was used frequently by Mohammed. Not one person in Arabia who opposed or criticized Mohammed lived except by fleeing or converting. Assassinations were common and feared.

B4,52,265 Mohammed ordered a band of Helpers to assassinate Abu Rafi. One of the group, Abdullah, slipped into his house at night and killed him in his sleep."

All Kafirs who resist in any way can be killed as an act of jihad.

B4,52,286 Mohammed was traveling one time when a Kafir spy came to him. After sitting and talking a while with Mohammed and his companions, the spy departed. Mohammed said, "Chase him down and kill him." So, I [Al Akwa] did. Mohammed rewarded me with the spy's possessions and his share of the spoils.

Captives could be killed or ransomed.

B4,53,367 Speaking about the captives from the battle of Badr, Mohammed said, "If Al-Mutim were alive and if he asked me to, I would have freed those people for his sake."

No death is too painful or fearful for the Kafir. Allah will be even more cruel in Hell for eternity.

B8,82,795 Mohammed punished the men of the Uraina tribe by cutting off their hands and feet and letting them bleed to death.

Here we see that Mohammed used propaganda as one of Islam's most valuable weapons of jihad. Allah supports propaganda and the debasement of Kafirs.

B5,59,449 Mohammed said to Hassan, "Insult them [the Kafirs] with your poetry and Gabriel will protect you."

M031,6074 Mohammed said, "Hassan B. Thibit, satirize and mock the Kafir; Gabriel is by your side." This hadith was narrated with the authority of Shu'ba and the same line of transmitters.

Jihad is the only sure path to Paradise.

B9,93,549 Mohammed said, "Allah promises that the Muslim who participates in jihad with no compulsion, other than true faith and the desire to serve Allah, will either be admitted into Paradise, or sent home with Allah's reward or a share of the spoils of war."

The poetry of this hadith is the most elegant expression of jihad.

B4,52,73 Mohammed: "Be aware that Paradise lies under the shadow of swords."

Jihad should be waged at the right time. Haste should never be a priority.

B4,52,86 Mohammed: "When you prepare to fight your enemy, take your time."

This is the Sunna of Mohammed

THE TEARS OF JIHAD

CHAPTER 4

These figures are a rough estimate of the death of Kafirs by the political act of jihad found in the Hadith.

AFRICANS

Thomas Sowell estimates that 11 million slaves were shipped across the Atlantic and 14 million were sent to the Islamic nations of North Africa and the Middle East[1]. For every slave captured many others died. Estimates of this collateral damage vary. The renowned missionary David Livingstone estimated that for every slave who reached the plantation five others died by being killed in the raid or died on the forced march from illness and privation[2]. So, for 25 million slaves delivered to the market, we have the death of about 120 million people. Islam ran the wholesale slave trade in Africa.[3]

120 million Africans

CHRISTIANS

The number of Christians martyred by Islam is 9 million[4]. A rough estimate by Raphael Moore in *History of Asia Minor* is that another 50 million died in wars by jihad. So to account for the 1 million African Christians killed in the 20th century we have:

60 million Christians

JEWS

The Jews had no political control over any country and their deaths were limited to a few thousand killed in riots.

---

1.   Thomas Sowell, *Race and Culture*, BasicBooks, 1994, p. 188.
2.   Woman's Presbyterian Board of Missions, *David Livingstone,* p. 62, 1888.
3   Bernard Lewis, *Race and Slavery in the Middle East*, Oxford University Press, 1990.
4.   David B. Barrett, Todd M. Johnson, *World Christian Trends AD 30-AD 2200*, William Carey Library, 2001, p. 230, table 4-10.

THE TEARS OF JIHAD

HINDUS

Koenard Elst in *Negationism in India*[5] gives an estimate of 80 million Hindus killed in the total jihad against India. The country of India today is only half the size of ancient India, due to jihad. The mountains near India are called the Hindu Kush, meaning the "funeral pyre of the Hindus".

80 million Hindus

BUDDHISTS

Buddhists do not keep up with the history of war. Keep in mind that in jihad only Christians and Jews were allowed to survive as dhimmis (second-class subjects under Sharia); everyone else had to convert or die. Jihad killed the Buddhists in Turkey, Afghanistan, along the Silk Route, and in India. The total is roughly 10 million[6].

10 million Buddhists

TOTAL

This gives a rough estimate of *270 million* killed by jihad.

---

5. Koenard Elst, *Negationism in India*, Voice of India, New Delhi, 2002, pg. 34.
6. David B. Barrett, Todd M. Johnson, *World Christian Trends AD 30-AD 2200*, William Carey Library, 2001, p. 230, table 4-1.

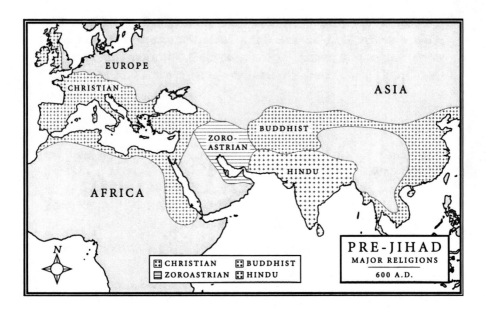

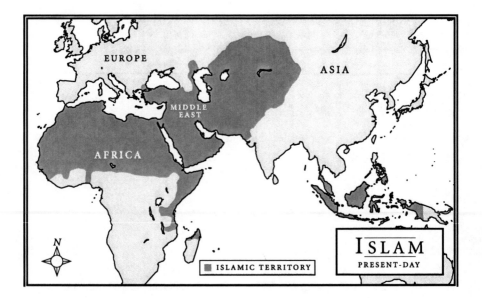

THE DHIMMIS

CHAPTER 5

*5:92 Obey Allah, and obey the Messenger, and be on your
guard. If you do turn back, know that our Messenger
is only bound to deliver a plain announcement.*

Mohammed took his army a hundred miles from Medina to Khaybar and attacked the Jews. Islam was totally victorious. After taking the property of the Jews as the spoils of war, the Muslims made an agreement called a *dhimma* with the Jews in Arabia. The Jews could stay and farm the land if they gave Islam half their profits. They then became *dhimmis* who were under the protection of Islam.

Thus the word dhimmi came to mean permanent, second-class Kafir subjects in a country ruled by Islam. Dhimmis paid a special tax, and their civil and legal rights were greatly limited. The only way out of being a dhimmi was to convert to Islam or flee. The taxes from the dhimmis made Islam rich.

There are very few hadiths about dhimmis, but it was another of Mohammed's unique political inventions. The scorched-earth policy of killing all Kafirs was satisfying to the warrior, but it had an inherent problem: once everyone was killed, the warrior had to find other work. Mohammed therefore created the policy of the dhimmi to deal with the Jews. Dhimmi status was expanded later to include Christians, Magians, and others.

Dual ethics is at the very core of the concept of a dhimmi. Political subjugation of Kafirs can only come about by viewing them as separate and apart from Allah's true human beings, Muslims.

It can be argued that the glory of Islam came not from Islam but its dhimmis' wealth and knowledge. The dhimmis were the scholars, since the Arabs of Mohammed's day were barely literate and their classical literature was oral poetry. The secular knowledge of Islam came from the Christians, Persians, Jews and Hindus.

Islam is credited with saving the knowledge of the Greeks from extinction. This is ironic in two ways. First, it was the jihad against the Byzantine/Greek culture that caused its collapse. Secondly, it was the Syrian Christian dhimmis who translated all of the Greek philosophers into Arabic.

The Hindu numbering system was credited to Islam. The Muslims took the zero from Hindu mathematicians, and today we call our numbers Arabic numerals. From carpets to architecture, the Muslims took the ideas of the dhimmis and obtained historical credit. The lists of great Islamic scholars includes the dhimmis with Arabic names living under Islamic dominance.

Over time, as the dhimmi population decreased, the "Golden Age" of Islam disappeared.

The dhimmis produced the wealth of Islam.

B4,53,388 Juwairiya said to Umar, "Oh, Caliph, give us your advice." Umar said, "You should continue the arrangement made by Mohammed regarding the dhimmis because the taxes they pay fund your children's future."

Dhimmitude is privation.

B4,53,380 Umar drove all the Kafirs from Arabia. After Mohammed conquered Khaybar, he considered expelling the Jews from the land of Allah, Mohammed and the Muslims. However, the Jews asked Mohammed if they could stay in exchange for their servitude and half of each harvest. Mohammed said, "You may stay on those terms as long as it pleases us." The Jews remained until Caliph Umar drove them from Arabia.

After jihad comes dhimmitude: Jihad cracks open the culture; dhimmitude replaces it with Islam. Afghanistan was a Buddhist nation until conquered by Islam; Pakistan was Hindu; Egypt was the culture of the Pharaohs even though it had become Christian; and North Africa was Christian.

It was Umar II who set the standards for dhimmis. His treaty states:

> We shall not build, in our cities or in their neighborhood new monasteries, churches, convents, or monks' cells, nor shall we repair, by day or by night, such of them as fall in ruins or are situated in the quarters of the Muslims.
>
> We shall keep our gates wide open for passersby and travelers. We shall give board and lodging to all Muslims who pass our way for three days.
>
> We shall not give shelter in our churches or in our dwellings to any spy nor hide him from the Muslims.
>
> We shall not manifest our religion publicly nor convert anyone to it. We shall not prevent any of our kin from entering Islam if they wish it.
>
> We shall show respect toward the Muslims, and we shall rise from our seats when they wish to sit.
>
> We shall not seek to resemble the Muslims by imitating any of their garments.

We shall not mount on saddles, nor shall we gird swords nor bear any kind of arms nor carry them on our persons.

We shall not engrave Arabic inscriptions on our seals.

We shall not sell fermented drinks.

We shall clip the fronts of our heads (keep a short forelock as a sign of humiliation).

We shall always dress in the same way wherever we may be, and we shall bind the zunar round our waists.

We shall not display our crosses or our books in the roads or markets of the Muslims. We shall only use clappers in our churches very softly. We shall not raise our voices when following our dead. We shall not take slaves who have been allotted to Muslims.

We shall not build houses higher than the houses of the Muslims.

Whoever strikes a Muslim with deliberate intent shall forfeit the protection of this pact.

(from Al-Turtushi, *Siraj Al-Muluk*, p. 229-30)

But this excerpt can not really describe the world of the dhimmi. Islam dominated all public space. The government was Islamic; the education was Islamic; dress was Islamic; literature was Islamic. Only inside the dhimmi's house could there be no Islam. The word of a dhimmi could not be used in court against a Muslim and crimes against dhimmis were rarely prosecuted.

The actual attitude of Islam toward the dhimmis was more contempt than hatred, and over time the dhimmis disappeared. They either left or converted. It was too hard to be a second-class subject, and the extra taxes were a burden. As time went on both Christians and Jews became more Arabic in their outlook; they started to treat women as the Arabs did and their customs became more and more Islamic. Finally it was easier to accept Islam as their religion and stop all the pressure and contempt.

This is the Sunna of Mohammed

THE JEWS

CHAPTER 6

*48:13 We have prepared a blazing Fire for these Kafirs
who do not believe in Allah and His Messenger.*

In Islam's early days, Mohammed began to preach in Mecca where there were a few Jews and a handful of Christians. At first Mohammed's god had no name, but soon it was called Rahman and, then, Allah. There had been a moon god called Allah in Arabia since the dawn of time. Allah was the chief god of the Quraysh, Mohammed's tribe, and Mohammed's father was called Abdullah, slave of Allah. Mohammed said his was the only god and identified Allah with the One-God of the Jews, Jehovah.

Mohammed claimed to be the last in the line of Jewish prophets. The stories in the Koran resembled the Jews' stories of Adam, Moses, Noah, and other figures in Jewish tradition. The Meccans had a great deal of respect for the Jews because they had a sacred text. Indeed, both Jews and Christians were called People of the Book. None of the Arabian religions had a religious book as the native Arabic religions were tribal and based on oral traditions.

Then Mohammed went to Medina. Half of Medina was Jewish. Their leaders did not agree with Mohammed that he was a Jewish prophet. The revelations of the Koran took on a different tone about the Jews. Their scriptures did not agree with Mohammed's, therefore their scriptures were wrong. Clearly they had changed them to oppose Mohammed. Less than two years later, there were no Jews left in Medina, and the Muslims had their possessions.

DEMEANING HADITHS

B1,12,749 Mohammed: "Say Amen when the Imam says, 'not the path of those who anger You [the Jews] nor the path of those who go astray [the Christians]' everyone who says Amen will have their past sins forgiven."

> 1:1 *In the name of Allah, the Most Gracious, the Most Merciful*
> *In the Name of Allah, the Compassionate, the Merciful.*
> *Praise be to Allah, Lord of the worlds.*
> *The Compassionate, the Merciful. King of the Judgment Day.*
> *Only You do we worship, and to You alone do we ask for help.*

Keep us on the straight and narrow path.
The path of those that You favor; not the path of those who anger
You [the Jews] nor the path of those who go astray [the Christians].
[This sura is repeated every day by Muslims.]

B2,23,457 While walking after dark, Mohammed heard a mournful cry and said, "Jews are being punished in the afterlife."

Mohammed claimed the mantle of all the Jewish prophets. He claimed that Allah was Jehovah and that all religious truth came through Allah. Islam has the best claim to Moses.

B3,31,222 After coming to Medina, Mohammed witnessed the Jews observing a fast on the day of Ashura. Asked about that, they said, "This is a holy day. It celebrates the day God delivered the Jews from their enemy. Moses fasted this day." Mohammed told them, "Muslims have more right to claim Moses as a prophet than you do." Consequently, Mohammed fasted that day and required all Muslims to fast on that day.

Jews lie.

B3,41,599 Mohammed said anyone who lies under oath with the aim to illegally take a Muslim's property will face Allah's wrath. Al-AshAth said, "That statement pertained to me. A Jew and I shared some common land, and he had denied that I was co-owner of the property. I took the dispute before Mohammed, who asked if I had proof of ownership. I said that I did not. Mohammed then asked the Jew to swear an oath that he was the rightful owner of the land. I said, "Mohammed, he will swear a false oath and steal my land." Therefore, Allah revealed this verse to Mohammed:

> 3:77 *Those who sell their covenant with Allah and their oaths for a meager price will have no part in the world to come.*

B4,56,662 Mohammed said, "You will imitate the sinful behavior of your ancestors so utterly and completely that if they did something stupid, you would do exactly the same thing."

We asked, "Are you talking about the Jews and the Christians?"

He answered, "Who else could I be talking about but the Jews and the Christians?"

B4,56,664 Aisha despised the practice of praying with hands on the flanks because that was the way the Jews used to pray.

B4,56,668 Mohammed: "When the head of a Jew or a Christian becomes gray, they refuse to dye their hair. You must do the opposite of their behavior. Therefore, dye your hair and beard when they become gray."

B6,60,157 Mohammed: "May Allah curse the Jews! Allah ordered them to not eat animal fat, so what do they do? They melt it down, sell it, and invest the proceeds."

Jews are the cause of decay and rebellious wives.

B4,55,547 Mohammed: "If it weren't for the Jews, meat would not rot. If not for Eve, wives would never disobey their mates."

B2,23,376 As Mohammed walked past a weeping family of Jews at their daughter's funeral, he said, "They are crying for her and she is being tortured in the grave."

M037,6666 Mohammed: "Allah will use a Christian or Jew to substitute for a Muslim in Hell."

Some rats are changed Jews.

M042,7135 Mohammed: "A tribe of Bani Isra'il [Jews] disappeared. I do not know what became of them, but I think they mutated and became rats. Have you noticed that a rat won't drink camel's milk, but it will drink goat's milk?"

Women as the spoils of war.

B5,59,512 During the night, just outside Khaybar, Mohammed gave the Fajr Prayer and said, "Allah is great! Khaybar will be in ruins. When we attack a city that has been warned, those people are in for an evil morning." As the people of Khaybar fled the city, Mohammed ordered the men killed and the women and children enslaved.

Safiya was amongst the captives. She first was the slave of Dahya but later on she belonged to Mohammed. Mohammed made the price of her freedom her wedding dowry.

To be protected from Islam, the Jew must submit to Islam.

B9,92,447 We were at the Mosque one day when Mohammed came out and said, "Let's go talk to the Jews."

When we arrived at their village, Mohammed addressed them saying, "Jews, submit to Allah. Become Muslim and you will be protected."

They answered, "You have delivered Allah's word, Mohammed."

Mohammed said, "That is my wish, accept Islam and you will be protected."

They repeated, "You have delivered Allah's word."

Mohammed said for a third time, "That is my wish; accept Islam and you will be protected," before adding, "You need to know that the Earth belongs to Allah, and I intend to expel you from this land. If you have property, you should sell it; otherwise, you had better remember that this land belongs to Allah and Mohammed."

B4,52,68 During the battle of the Trench, Mohammed paused from fighting, stripped off his weapons, and bathed. Gabriel, covered in dust, revealed himself to Mohammed and said, "You have laid down your weapons. I have not laid my arms down yet."

Mohammed asked, "Where do you want me to go?"

Gabriel said, "That way," pointing toward the Jewish camp.

Mohammed armed himself and marched into battle.

When the Jews of Fadak heard what had happened to the Jews of Khaybar, they surrendered before they were even attacked by Mohammed.

B4,52,153 Because the property of the Jews that Allah had given to Mohammed had not been won by the Muslims through the use of their horses and camels, it belonged exclusively to Mohammed. Mohammed used it to give his family their yearly allowance and he spent the rest on weapons and horses for jihad.

The Last Days

B4,52,176 Mohammed: Muslims will fight with the Jews until some of them will hide behind stones. The stones will betray them saying, "Slave of Allah, there is a Jew hiding behind me; kill him."

This is the Sunna of Mohammed

CHRISTIANS

CHAPTER 7

4:115 Anyone who opposes the Messenger after having
received Our guidance and follows a path other than
that of the true believer will be left to their own devices.
We will lead them into Hell, an evil home.

The Koran says that Christians who submit to Islam can go to Paradise. Every reference to Christians in the Hadith is negative.

A Muslim repeats the following verses daily:

1:5 Only You do we worship, and to You alone do we ask for help.
Keep us on the straight and narrow path. The path of those that
You favor; not the path of those who anger You [the Jews] nor the
path of those who go astray [the Christians].

B1,12,749 Mohammed: "Say Amen when the Imam guides you along the right path and says, 'not the path of the Jews who deserve your anger, nor the way of the Christians who have gone astray.' All of a Muslim's past sins are forgiven when they say Amen in concert with the angels."

The Christians and Jews who reject Mohammed will go to Hell.

M001,0284 Mohammed: "According to Allah, any Jew or Christian that is aware of me, but dies before accepting my prophecy will be sent to Hell."

Religious apartheid in Arabia.

B3,39,531 Upon the death of Mohammed, Umar drove the Jews and Christians out of Arabia. Mohammed had intended to do so after he had conquered Khaybar, as the land then became the possession of Allah, Mohammed, and the Muslims. Mohammed granted their request to remain, however, in exchange for their labor and half of the proceeds. Mohammed said, "You may stay under those conditions for as long as we allow it." Thus they remained until Umar expelled them from Arabia.

B4,56,662 Mohammed warned the people, "You will follow the errant path of those who came before you so completely, that if they did a stupid thing, you would too." The people asked, "Mohammed, do you mean the Christians and the Jews?" He answered, "Whom else would I mean?"

The very earth rejects those who criticize Islam and Mohammed.

B4,56,814 Once there was a Christian who accepted Islam, studied the Koran, and wrote down Allah's revelations to Mohammed. The man later reverted back to Christianity and would say, "Mohammed doesn't know anything except what I have written down for him."

After the man died and was buried, his friends found his body disinterred. They said, "This is the work of Mohammed and his followers. They have pulled him from his grave because he rejected them."

The man's friends dug another, deeper grave and reburied their friend. The next day, however, the man's body was again found thrown from the grave.

His friends again blamed Mohammed and his companions for the act and proceeded to dig another, even deeper grave.

In the morning, the man's friends again found the grave empty and the body thrown on the ground. The man's friends were then convinced that the earth had rejected the man's body and that humans were not to blame, so they left the body on the ground.

M033,6423 Mohammed: "No one is born that is not created according to his true nature. A parent turns his child into a Jew, Christian, or pagan, just as an animal produces an offspring that imitates itself." He then quoted the Koran, "Allah creates man according to his natural state. There can be no alteration by man to what Allah has created. This natural state is the correct religion."

M037,6666 Mohammed: "Allah will fill a Muslim's place in Hell with a Christian or a Jew."

Muslims believe the Christian scriptures were corrupted to conceal the truth about the superior religion of Islam and Mohammed's superiority to Christ.

B3, 48, 850 Ibn Abbas: "Muslims, why do you ask the Jews and Christians any questions? The Koran that was revealed to Mohammed contains the latest word from Allah. It has not been altered and you recite it daily. Allah has made clear to you that the Jews and the Christians have distorted the Scriptures that were revealed to them. They have claimed that their alterations are the word of God in order to achieve some material gain."

This is the Sunna of Mohammed

SLAVES

CHAPTER 8

4:42 On that day the Kafirs and those who disobeyed
the Messenger will wish they could sink into the earth
for they cannot hide a single thing from Allah.

Islam has a complete set of laws concerning slavery. Here are some of the hadiths that form the basis of these Islamic laws. The ethical system of slavery is pure dual ethics.

RULES, REGULATIONS

The treatment of a slave includes beatings.
B7,62,132 Mohammed: "Nobody should beat his wife as he would a slave and then have sex with her that night."

M001,0131 Mohammed: "If a slave flees his master, Allah does not hear his prayer."

B3,34,362 Mohammed: "If it is proven that a slave girl has had illegal sex, her master should whip her but should not continue to fault her after she is punished. If it should again be proved that she had illegal sex, her master should whip her but should not fault her after the legal punishment. If she should commit the infraction for a third time, he should sell her for even the smallest price."

B3,46,723 Mohammed: "Any man that educates his slave girl, teaches her etiquette, grants her freedom, and then marries her will receive a double reward in Paradise. Any slave that accepts Allah's and his owner's mastery will be doubly rewarded in Paradise."

B3,48,827 Uqba married a woman named Um Yahya. He said, "A black slave woman came to me and said, 'I wet-nursed you and your wife.'" I told Mohammed about this and he turned his head. I walked around and looked him in the face and he said, "How can you remain married to Um Yahya when you know that you both suckled at the same breast?" Mohammed ordered Uqba to divorce Um Yahya.

B3,36,483 Mohammed banned the practice of using slave girls as prostitutes.

B3,46,702 Ibn Umar gave similar verdicts in disputes centering on slaves owned by more than one master, where one owner wished to free the slave from his share of bondage. In cases like that Umar would say, "The slave owner who wishes to free a slave from his share of bondage should completely free the slave if he has the resources to fairly compensate the other owner(s). The other owners should accept the fair price and free the slave."

SLAVES IN THE DAILY LIFE OF ISLAM

Slaves are as common as camels in the Hadith, Sira, and Koran. Here are some selections that show the ubiquity of slaves in everyday life.

B2,15,103 During the days of Mina, Abu Bakr visited Aisha. While Mohammed was lying down, two young slave girls were beating a tambourine. Abu Bakr yelled at them to stop their noise. Mohammed uncovered his face and told Abu Bakr, "Leave them alone. It's the days of 'Id and the days of Mina [festival days]."

Aisha also said, "One time Mohammed was hiding me from public view so that I might watch some black slaves in the Mosque display their skill with weapons.

Umar scolded them for exhibiting themselves in the presence of a Muslim woman, but Mohammed said, "Leave them alone. You Negroes may continue; you have my protection."

B3,27,22 Asma's slave Abdullah once told me that he could hear Asma when she would walk by Al-Hajun. She would say, "May Allah bless His messenger Mohammed."

B3,38,500 We used to graze sheep at Sala. One time, one of our slave-girls saw a dying sheep. She chipped a rock and used it to kill and butcher the animal. My father told everyone, "Don't eat that meat until I speak to Mohammed." My father asked Mohammed if the meat was permissible to eat, and he said that it was. Ubaidullah said, "I admire that girl. Even though she is a slave, she had the courage to slaughter that sheep."

B3,47,743 Mohammed sent for an Immigrant woman who owned a slave skilled in carpentry. Mohammed said to her, "Order your slave to build a pulpit." She did so, and he built a pulpit of tamarisk wood. Upon completion, it was brought to Mohammed who personally lifted and situated the pulpit where you now see it.

B5,58,262 The first Muslims to emigrate from Mecca to Medina were MusAb and Ibn Um Maktum, who taught the Koran to the Helpers. Next came Umar and twenty other followers of Mohammed. When Mohammed came to Medina, he said, "I had never seen the people so happy. Even the slave girls were shouting, 'Mohammed is here!'"

B8,73,229 Mohammed was traveling one time and slave called Anjasha was urging the camels to run faster. Mohammed said, "Anjasha, drive the camels with the fine glassware more slowly." By fine glassware, he meant the female passengers.

MOHAMMED AND SLAVERY

Islam has the most developed religious attitude, legal framework, social theory, and customs regarding slavery. The term *slave* is a positive one in Islam. Mohammed referred to himself and Muslims as the "slaves of Allah." Mohammed's second convert was a slave.

Mohammed himself was involved in every single aspect of slavery. He had non-believing men killed so that the surviving women and children could be made slaves[1]; he owned many slaves, some of them black,[2] and he gave slaves away for gifts;[3] he passed around slaves for the purpose of sex to men who were his chief lieutenants.[4] Mohammed stood by while others beat slaves;[5] he captured slaves and wholesaled them to raise money for jihad.[6] He shared the pleasure of sex with the captured women after conquest.[7] One of his favorite sexual partners was a slave who bore him a son.[8] He got slaves as gifts from other rulers.[9] The very pulpit that he preached from was made by a slave.[10] He ate food prepared by slaves.[11] He was treated medically by a slave[12]. Mohammed had a slave tailor[13]. He declared that a slave who ran away from his master would not

1. Guillaume, *Life of Mohammed*, 466.
2. Ibid., 516.
3. Ibid., 499.
4. Ibid., 593.
5. Ibid., 295.
6. Ibid., 466.
7. Ibid, 496.
8. William Muir, *The Life of Mohammed* (New York: AMS Press, 1975), 425.
9. Ibid.
10. Bukhari, Hadith, Volume 1, Book 8, Number 440.
11. Ibid., Volume 3, Book 34, Number 295.
12. Ibid., Volume 3, Book 36, Number 481.
13. Ibid., Volume 7, Book 65, Number 344.

have his prayers answered.[14] He approved an owner's having sex with his slaves.[15] He called himself a slave of Allah.

BLACKS

Blacks are mentioned in passing in the hadiths, usually in a negative tone. Mohammed frequently used the term *raisin head* for Ethiopians and Africans.

B1,11,662 Mohammed: "Obey and listen to your ruler, even if he is an Ethiopian with a head like a raisin."

Blacks will do evil in the future to Islam.

B2,26,661 Mohammed: "An Ethiopian with two skinny legs will destroy the Kabah."

B9,87,163 Mohammed: "In a dream I saw a black woman with messy hair leaving Medina to live in Mahaia. I think that it meant that an epidemic would begin in Medina and would be spread to Mahaia."

B4,52,309 My [Rafi's] grandfather asked Mohammed, "We may engage the enemy tomorrow, but we have no knives. How shall we slaughter our animals?"

Mohammed answered, "If you invoke Allah's name beforehand and you use a tool that causes profuse bleeding, then you may eat. However, do not use a tooth or a nail to slaughter an animal. A tooth is the same as a bone, and it is forbidden to slaughter with a bone. You should not use a nail because that is what the Ethiopians (Africans) use, and we don't want to copy them."

This is the Sunna of Mohammed

---

14. Muslim, Hadith, Book 001, Number 0131.
15. Ibid., Book 008, Number 3383.

WOMEN

CHAPTER 9

*3:131 Obey Allah and His messenger so
that you may receive mercy.*

There are many references in the Hadith to women and their place in the world.

HELL

Most of those in Hell will be women.

B1,2,28 Mohammed said, "I have seen the fires of Hell and most of its residents are ungrateful women." He was asked, "Are they Kafirs, or did they show ingratitude to Allah?" He answered, "They were not grateful to their husbands and not grateful for the kindness shown them."

Women are inferior to men in intelligence and religion.

B1,6,301 While on his way to pray, Mohammed passed a group of women and he said, "Ladies, give to charities and donate money to the unfortunate, because I have witnessed that most of the people in Hell are women.

They asked, "Why is that?"

He answered, "You swear too much, and you show no gratitude to your husbands. I have never come across anyone more lacking in intelligence, or ignorant of their religion than women. A careful and intelligent man could be misled by many of you."

They responded, "What exactly are we lacking in intelligence or faith?"

Mohammed said, "Is it not true that the testimony of one man is the equal to the testimony of two women?"

After they affirmed that this was true, Mohammed said, "That illustrates that women are lacking in intelligence. Is it not also true that women may not pray nor fast during their menstrual cycle?" They said that this was also true.

Mohammed then said, "That illustrates that women are lacking in their religion."

Women are ingrates.

B2,18,161 During the life of Mohammed, there was a solar eclipse. Mohammed gave the special eclipse prayer and stood upright for a long time. He then alternately bowed and stood for long periods of time before prostrating himself and finishing the prayer. When he had finished, the eclipse had ended.

Mohammed said, "The moon and the sun are two signs of Allah. They are not eclipsed because of the birth or death of someone. When you look at them, think of Allah."

Some people said, "Mohammed, we saw you reach out to something and then retreat."

Mohammed answered, "I witnessed Paradise, and I reached out my hand toward some wonderful fruit that grows there. If I had been able to return with that fruit, you might have eaten it until the end of time. I also witnessed the fires of Hell. Never have I seen such a dreadful sight. Furthermore, most of the people there were female."

The people wondered, "Why was that?"

Mohammed responded, "Because of their ingratitude." When he was asked if it was because they were ungrateful to Allah, Mohammed said, "No, it is because of their ingratitude toward their husbands and for their ingratitude for the good things they were blessed with. You could be kind and benevolent to a woman all of her life, but if she sees one fault in you, she will say, 'You have never been good to me.'"

SEX

M008,3367 Mohammed: "If a man wishes to bed his wife and she refuses, Allah will be displeased with her until her husband is pleased with her."

The man gets exile and one hundred lashes for adultery; the woman is killed.

B3,49,860 A nomad and another man came before Mohammed, seeking his solution to a dispute.

The nomad said, "Mohammed, use Islamic law to settle our dispute." The other man said, "Yes, we will abide by Allah's law as you dictate."

The nomad began, "My son worked for this man and he fornicated with the man's wife. Some people said that he must be stoned to death; to save him from that punishment, I paid a penalty of one hundred sheep and one slave girl. Then I asked some Islamic scholars who said, 'Your son must be given one-hundred lashes and be exiled one year.'"

Mohammed said, "I will settle this dispute using Allah's law. Your son must be exiled for one year, and he must be lashed one hundred times. The slave-girl and the one hundred sheep will be returned to you." Mohammed then turned to a companion and said, "Unais, seize this man's wife. She must be stoned to death." Consequently, Unais went and stoned the woman to death.

CLEAN/UNCLEAN

B1,4,228 Fatima asked Mohammed, "My uterus bleeds persistently. I can't remain clean. Must I forsake praying?" Mohammed said, "No. The bleeding is caused by blood vessels, not your menses. When your cycle begins, refrain from prayer. When the cycle is over, take a bath and resume prayers."

INFERIOR STATUS

B2,20,192 Mohammed: "A woman should not travel for more than three days unless accompanied by her husband, or a man whom she cannot marry, like her father, brother, or grandfather."

M031,5966 Mohammed: "There are many perfect men, but the only perfect women are Mary, the daughter of Imran, Asiya, the wife of Pharaoh, and Aisha (Mohammed's favorite wife). The superiority of Aisha to other women is like comparing Tharid [an unknown reference] to other foods."

B2,20,194 Mohammed: "A woman who believes in Allah and the Day of Reckoning may not travel for more than one day unaccompanied by a close male relative."

M036,6603 Mohammed: "After I am gone, the biggest threat to stability that will remain is the harm done to men by women."

B3,31,172 Mohammed: "Is it not a fact that women do not pray or fast during menstruation? That is the deficiency in her religion."

B6,60,51 The Jews used to have an old saying, "If during sex you enter your wife from behind, then your child will have squinty eyes." Consequently, Allah revealed this verse to Mohammed:

> 2:223 Your women are your plowed fields: go into your fields when you like, but do some good deed beforehand and fear Allah. Keep in mind that you will meet Him. Give good news to the believers.

B3,48,826 Mohammed asked, "Is not the value of a woman's eye-witness testimony half that of a man's?" A woman said, "Yes." He said, "That is because a woman's mind is deficient."

B7,62,31 Mohammed: "If anything can be a bad sign, it would be a house, a horse, or a woman."

B7,62,33 Mohammed: "After I die, the biggest problem that I leave to man is woman."

B7,62,113 Mohammed: "A woman is like a rib; if you try to straighten her out, she will break. To get any benefit from her, you must leave her crooked."

Old age of women is a reason for divorce in Islam. When one of Mohammed's wives turned forty she made an arrangement to stay in Mohammed's harem because his wives were guaranteed Paradise, but she gave up sex.

B7,62,134 Concerning the verse:

> 4:128 *And if a wife fears cruelty or desertion from her husband, then they are not to blame for coming to a mutual agreement between themselves, for peace is best, although people are often prone to greed.*

Allah's statement pertains to the man who wishes to divorce his wife and marry another. His wife asks him not to divorce her, but rather keep her without any compulsion to have sex with her or provide for her.

An abused, beaten, and bruised woman appeared in front of Mohammed.

B7,72,715 Upon her divorce from Rifaa, a woman married Abdur Rahman. Soon after she went to Aisha, wearing a green veil, and complained of her new husband's brutality, showing her the discolored bruises on her skin.

Aisha interceded on her behalf with Mohammed saying, "I have never witnessed women being mistreated as much as Muslim women. Look at her bruises. She has been beaten greener than the veil she wears."

When Abdur Rahman learned that his new wife had complained to Mohammed about his behavior, he went to the prophet accompanied by his two sons from a previous marriage. His wife said, "I have done this man no wrong. Furthermore, he is impotent and as good to me as this floppy fringe that hangs from my robe."

Abdur Rahman responded, "She lies. I am very virile and can satisfy her, but she doesn't obey me and she wants to remarry Rifaa."

Mohammed told the woman, "If that is your wish, you should know that is illegal for you to remarry Rifaa if you have not had sex with Abdur

Rahman. Mohammed then looked to the two boys accompanying Abdur Rahman and asked, "Are these your boys?"

Abdur Rahman said, "Yes."

Mohammed then said to the woman, "You say he is impotent? Those boys look just like him."

CREATURES OF PLEASURE

Kafir women are for the pleasure of Muslim men, and forced sex with captives is approved.

B5,59,459 Entering the Mosque, Ibn Muhairiz saw Abu Said and asked him whether *coitus interruptus* is sanctified by Allah.

Abu Said said, "Accompanying Mohammed at the battle of Banu Al-Mustaliq, we were rewarded with Arab captives, including several woman who were very sought-after because celibacy had become quite a hardship. We had planned to practice *coitus interruptus* [when sold as slaves later, the women would bring a lesser price if pregnant] but felt that we should seek instruction first from Mohammed.

Mohammed said, however, "It is better that you not interrupt copulation to prevent pregnancy because if a soul is predestined to exist, then it will exist."

MARRIAGE

The most important part of a woman is her vagina.

B7,62,81 Mohammed said, "The marriage vow most rightly expected to be obeyed is the husband's right to enjoy the wife's vagina."

B7,62,121 Mohammed: "If a woman refuses her husband's request for sex, the angels will curse her through the night."

TEMPORARY MARRIAGE

A unique custom of Islam is temporary marriage. For an amount of money, a man can sleep with a woman for three days. Shia Islam still has this custom.

B7,62,51 Abu Jamra witnessed Ibn Abbas deliver a verdict permitting temporary marriages between jihadists and eligible women. Upon hearing this verdict, a freed slave of Ibn Abbas asked, "This is only permitted if it is really necessary and woman are hard to come by, correct?"

Ibn Abbas replied, "Yes."

B7,62,130 Abdullah said, "While on jihad with Mohammed, many of us did not have wives accompanying us. We asked whether we should get castrated?" Mohammed ordered us not to do that, and he gave us permission to take temporary wives before reciting this verse.

> 5:87 *O, you who believe, do not forbid the good things that Allah allows you, but do not commit excess for Allah does not love those who commit excess.*

M008,3248 We went to Jibir B. Abdullah's home when he came to perform Umra. There the people asked him about many things, among them the temporary marriage. He said, "Yes, we have enjoyed the temporary marriage while Mohammed was alive and also during the reigns of Abu Bakr and Umar."

RULES

B7,72,815 Allah's curse is on women that either give or receive tattoos; those that pluck their facial hair and those that do anything to alter their natural appearance. If such actions are cursed by Allah and Mohammed, why should I presume to treat such women differently? This is revealed in the Koran:

> 59:7 *...take what the Messenger has offered you, and refuse what he has forbidden you. And fear Allah, for Allah is severe in His punishment.*

B7,62,133 A woman from the Helpers had a daughter whose hair began to fall out soon after she became wed. The woman asked Mohammed his advice saying, "My daughter's husband suggests that she wear a wig." Mohammed said, "Don't let her do that. Allah curses women who wear artificial hair."

B3,38,508 Mohammed said, "Unais, confront this man's wife and if she admits committing adultery have her stoned to death."

B8,82,803 Ali had a woman stoned to death on a Friday and said, "I have punished her as Mohammed would have."

This is the Sunna of Mohammed

APOSTATES

*33:21 You have an excellent example in Allah's Messenger
for those of you who put your hope in Allah and the
Last Day and who praise Allah continually.*

In Islam the option of killing an apostate, one who leaves Islam, is spelled out the Hadith, the Sira, and the early history of Islam after Mohammed's death.

When Mohammed died, entire tribes wanted to leave Islam. The first wars fought by Islam were against these apostates, and thousands were killed.

B2,23,483 After the death of Mohammed, Abu Bakr became the caliph, and he declared war against a group of Arabs who reverted back to paganism.

Umar asked Abu Bakr, "How can you war against these men when you remember that Mohammed said, 'I have been ordered by Allah to continue the fight until all the people say, "There is no god except Allah," and whoever says this will have his life and possessions protected from my anger. The exceptions being legal regulations that are adjudicated by man; Allah will settle all accounts.

Abu Bakr said, "I will fight those who argue that no difference exists between the tax [the poor tax was a Muslim obligation] and the prayer. The tax is an obligation put upon man by Allah. If someone should refuse to pay me even the smallest amount that they used to pay during the time of Mohammed, then I will fight them for doing so."

Umar then said, "Allah spoke to Abu Bakr, and I now know that he was right."

B9,83,17 Mohammed: "A Muslim who has admitted that there is no god but Allah and that I am His prophet may not be killed except for three reasons: as punishment for murder, for adultery, or for reverting back to non-belief after accepting Islam."

B9,84,57 Ali ordered that some atheists brought before him be burnt to death. Upon hearing this, Ibn Abbas said, "If it were me, I would not have ordered them burnt. Mohammed told us, 'Don't punish people with fire. That is Allah's punishment.' I would have done as Mohammed instructed, 'Whoever turns his back on Islam, kill him.'"

Killing false Muslims is rewarded by Allah.

B9,84,64 If I [Ali] relate something to you that Mohammed said, I swear to Allah that I would rather be smashed to pieces than to put false words in his mouth. However, if I were to say something other than a Hadith to you, then it may very well be false because I may seek to trick my enemies.

Without question I heard Mohammed say, "In the final days there will be young fools who will say all the appropriate things, but their conviction won't go any further than their words, and they will flee their faith like an arrow flies from a bow. Wherever you find such people, kill them. Whoever kills them will be rewarded on Judgment day."

No punishment is too great for the apostate.

B8,82,797 Some people came to Medina and soon became ill, so Mohammed sent them to the place where the camels were sheltered and told them to drink camel urine and milk as a remedy. They followed his advice, but when they recovered, they killed the shepherd guarding the camels and stole the herd.

In the morning, Mohammed heard what the men had done and ordered their capture. Before noon, the men were captured and brought before Mohammed. He ordered that their hands and feet be cut off and their eyes gouged out with hot pokers. They were then thrown on jagged rocks, their pleas for water ignored and they died of thirst.

Abu said, "They were thieves and murderers who abandoned Islam and reverted to paganism, thus attacking Allah and Mohammed."

Kill the apostate.

B9,89,271 A certain Jew accepted Islam, but then reverted to his original faith. Muadh saw the man with Abu Musa and said, "What has this man done?"

Abu Musa answered, "He accepted Islam, but then reverted to Judaism."

Muadh then said, "It is the verdict of Allah and Mohammed that he be put to death and I'm not going to sit down unless you kill him." [Death is the sentence for apostasy, leaving Islam.]

This is the Sunna of Mohammed

SEX

CHAPTER 11

*8:20 Believers! Be obedient to Allah and His messenger, and
do not turn your backs now that you know the truth. Do
not be like the ones who say, "We hear," but do not obey.*

RULES ABOUT SEX

B1,4,143 Mohammed: "If, before having sex with his wife, a man says,
'In the name of Allah, shield us from Satan and protect the off-spring
of our union from Satan.' Then if it is ordained that a child should be
conceived, Satan will be powerless to harm that child."

M002,0566 After staying the night in Aisha's home, a man washed his
clothes after waking. Aisha told him, "If you saw some semen, washing
the spot would serve to purify the garment. If the spot was not visible,
then sprinkling water around it would suffice. When I see semen on
Mohammed's clothes, I merely scrape it off and he says a prayer while
getting dressed."

B1,5,280 Um Sulaim, Abu Talha's wife, went to Mohammed and asked,
"Mohammed, obviously, Allah does not shrink from speaking the truth
to you. Must a woman bathe after having a wet dream?" Mohammed
answered, "Yes, if she had a discharge."

B1,5,290 Mohammed: "When a man is encompassed by a woman and
has had sex with her, a ritual bath is necessary."

B8,74,312 Mohammed: "There are five things that prophets have in
common: circumcision, shaved pubic hair, plucked armpits, a closely
trimmed moustache, and trimmed finger nails."

SEXUAL MUTILATION

M037,6676 A man was accused of fornicating with one of Mohammed's
slave girls. Mohammed said to Ali, "Go and kill this man." Ali found the man
cooling himself in a well, and said, "Come out." When the man emerged
from the well, however, Ali noticed that the man had been castrated. Seeing

this, Ali spared the man's life. Ali returned to Mohammed and explained, "The man does not have a penis."

This hadith refers to the circumcision of female genitalia. The Sunna of Mohammed is that he never forbade the removal of the clitoris, a common custom of his day.

M003,0684 An argument arose in Medina between a group of Helpers and Immigrants concerning bathing. The Helpers believed that bathing after sex was obligatory only if there is an ejaculation. The Immigrants believed that a bath is always obligatory after sex. Abu Musa said, "Let me settle the matter." He went to Aisha and asked and received her permission to speak. He said, "Aisha, beloved of the prophet, I want to question you about an embarrassing matter." Aisha said, "Do not be shy. Speak to me as you would your mother." Abu Musa then said, "When is a bath obligatory?" Aisha responded, "You have asked the right person. Mohammed has said that a bath is obligatory when a man is encompassed by a woman and their circumcised genitalia touch."

JIHAD AND SEXUAL CONDUCT

B7,62,130 Several of us became sexually frustrated while on jihad with no women. We asked Mohammed whether we should castrate ourselves. He forbade us from that action, but he did give us permission to take a temporary wife, which we could have simply by giving a woman a garment." Abdullah then recited the Koran:

> 5:87 *O, you who believe, do not forbid the good things that Allah allows you, but do not commit excess for Allah does not love those who commit excess.*

Rape of a Kafir female captive is jihad.

B7,62,137 Receiving female slaves as shares of spoils of war, we would practice coitus interruptus with them to avoid unwanted pregnancy. We asked Mohammed his opinion, and he asked us three times, "Do you really remove yourself?" He then said, "No soul that is not preordained to exist will be created."

LAWS ABOUT SEX

B3,48,817 Mohammed ordered an unmarried man exiled for a year and that he be lashed one hundred times for having illegal sexual intercourse.

B3,49,860 A Bedouin and another man went to Mohammed and the Bedouin said, "Settle our dispute using the laws of Allah." The other man said, "Yes, let Allah's law settle our dispute." The Bedouin said, "My son worked for this man and had illegal sex with his wife. Some said that my son must be stoned to death. To save my son, I gave a ransom of one hundred sheep and a slave girl. Islamic scholars, however, said that my son must be lashed one hundred times and be exiled for a year." Mohammed said, "According to Allah's law, your son must be lashed one hundred times and be exiled for a year. The sheep and the slave girl must be returned to you." Mohammed then said, "Unais, seize that man's wife and stone her until she is dead." Unais then went and stoned the woman to death.

MISCELLANEOUS

B7,72,774 Mohammed cursed effeminate men and masculine women. He said, "Throw such people from your homes." Mohammed ordered such a man to be turned out and Umar ordered such a woman turned out.

B4,54,460 Mohammed: "If a man asks his wife for sex and she refuses, causing him to go to sleep angry, the angels will curse her the entire night."

M008,3363 Jabir said that the Jews had an expression which said, "When a man has sex with his wife from behind, their child will have squinty eyes." Consequently, the verse was revealed,

> 2:223 Your women are your plowed fields: go into your fields when you like, but do some good deed beforehand and fear Allah. Keep in mind that you will meet Him. Give good news to the believers.

M008,3365 Mohammed: "It is all right if a man wants to enter his wife from behind or from on top, but he should enter the vagina."

A Kafir captive woman could be used for sex even if she was married and her husband was present.

M008,3432 Abu Sa'id Al-Khudri relates that while Mohammed was at the Battle of Hunain he sent a detachment to Autas and defeated the enemy there. Although Mohammed's soldiers captured many females, they were reluctant to force sex with them because their husbands were polytheists. Allah, however, then revealed to them that it was permissible as soon as a woman's menstrual cycle ended.

SATAN AND SUPERSTITIONS

CHAPTER 12

47:33 Believers! Obey Allah and the messenger,
and do not let your effort be in vain.

MAGIC

B7,71,636 Mohammed said, "There is no disputing the existence of an evil eye." He also forbade tattooing.

SATAN

M023,5046 Mohammed: "Satan is with you in everything that you do. He is there when you are eating, therefore if you drop any food from your mouth, you should brush away any dirt and eat it. Do not leave any for Satan. When you finish eating, lick your fingers clean, because you do not know where the blessing resides in the food."

M024,5279 Mohammed: "The bell is Satan's musical instrument."

B4,54,492 Someone mentioned to Mohammed a man that slept long after sunrise. Mohammed said, "Satan has urinated in that man's ears."

B4,54,500 Mohammed: "At dusk, keep your children near, because the devil is out. After an hour they may roam. Invoke Allah's name and close your house gates at night. Invoke Allah's name and cover your dishes. If your dishes lack covers, then place some wood or something over them."

B4,54,509 Mohammed: "Satan causes yawning. If any of you yawn, stop as soon as you can. If you are yawning, before you know it, Satan will be causing you mischief."

B7,69,527 Mohammed: "At dusk, keep your children inside, because that is when the devils roam. After an hour of night, however, they may go to their rooms and you may invoke Allah and close your doors. Satan can not open a shut door. Invoke Allah and cap your water bottle; invoke Allah and cover your dishes. Cover them however you may, and turn out your lights."

JINNS AND SPIRITS

Jinns are nonmaterial creatures who can help and hurt humans. Humans are made from earth and jinns are made from fire. Jinns occur in the Koran as well; one sura is titled "The Jinns."

B4,54,533 Mohammed: "Put lids on your pots and pans, cover your dishes, and put the cap on the water bottle at night. Lock your doors and keep a close eye on your children at night because that is when the jinns run amuck. Upon going to bed, put out the lights so that a rat can't cause a fire and burn the house down."

B5,58,199 Masruq and I [Abdur-Rahman] were talking and I asked him, "Who told Mohammed about the jinns listening to the Koran?" He replied, "Your father, Abdullah, told me that Mohammed heard about them from a tree."

B5,58,200 One time, Mohammed asked, "Who are you?" I answered, "Abu Huraira." He said, "Get me some stones so I may wipe my anus, and take care that you don't bring me any dried dung or bone."

Later I asked him what was the significance of the bone and the dung and he said, "That is what jinns eat."

The jinn delegate from Nasibin—a very charming jinn—asked that they might have the residue from human food. I interceded with Allah for them that they might never be hungry as long as there was dung and bones for them to feed upon.

This is the Sunna of Mohammed

BODILY FUNCTIONS

CHAPTER 13

58:20 Those who oppose Allah and His
Messenger will be laid low.

Since Mohammed is the ideal pattern of Islam, and being a Muslim entails copying all his actions, the hadiths go into great detail about Mohammed's bodily functions. Here are a very few samples:

URINATION / DEFECATION

M002,0504 Salman testified that he was told: "You learn everything that you need to know from Mohammed, even about feces." Salman replied, "Yes. Mohammed has forbade us from facing the kiblah [Mecca] while defecating or urinating, or from wiping the anus with the right hand or wiping with fewer than three pebbles or with animal dung or a piece of bone."

B1,4,144 When Mohammed went to relieve himself, he would say, "Allah, protect me from evil spirits and from wicked actions."

B1,4,146 Mohammed: "If anyone must relieve themselves while in an open area, they should not face toward or away from Mecca. Instead, they should either turn to the west or the east."

B1,8,388 Mohammed said, "Do not face toward or away from Mecca while defecating. Instead face either west or east." Abu Aiyub also said, "Arriving in Sham, we found toilets facing Mecca. So, we used them, but turned our faces sideways and begged Allah to forgive us."

B1,4,147 It is commonly said, "While sitting and using the toilet, do not face Mecca." I [Abdullah] say to them, "One time, on the roof of my house, I saw Mohammed sitting on a couple of bricks while relieving himself. He was facing Jerusalem, but a screen shielded him."

B1,4,156 Mohammed: "Do not hold your penis or clean your genitals with your right hand. When drinking, do not breathe into the cup."

M003,0729 Upon entering a toilet, Mohammed would say: "Allah, protect me from that which is evil and foul smelling."

B1,4,163 Mohammed: "When performing ablution, a person should place water in his nostrils and blow it out. Anyone that wipes his anus with stones should use an odd number of stones. Upon waking, a person should wash his hands before performing ablution because no one knows where his hands have been while sleeping."

FLATULENCE

B1,4,137 Mohammed: "A person at prayer who either urinates, defecates, or breaks wind must repeat ablution, or his prayer will not be accepted."

B1,4,139 Mohammed was asked by my uncle about an acquaintance who suspected that he may have broken wind while praying. Mohammed said, "Unless he either hears or smells something, he should not stop praying."

B1,8,436 Mohammed: "As long as a person is properly praying and does not break wind, the angels will continue to ask Allah's forgiveness for you. The angels say, 'Allah be merciful. Forgive him.'"

B8,73,68 Mohammed outlawed laughing at someone for breaking wind.

SPITTING

B1,8,404 Mohammed: "Nobody should spit directly in front of himself or to his right, rather he should spit to his left or beneath his foot."

This is the Sunna of Mohammed

MEDICINE, HEALTH, SCIENCE

CHAPTER 14

3:32 Say: Obey Allah and His messenger, but if they reject it,
then truly, Allah does not love those who reject the faith.

SCIENCE

B4,54,421One day as the sun was setting, Mohammed asked me [Abu Dhar], "Do you know where the sun goes at night?" I said, "You and Allah know better than I." Mohammed said, "It travels until it sits under the throne of Allah where it waits until permission is given to rise. A day will come when the sun will not be allowed to rest, nor continue on its regular path. It will instead be ordered to return the way it came and will rise in the west. That is how I interpret Allah's revelation:

> *36:37 The night is a sign for them. We withdraw it from the day and*
> *plunge them into darkness, and the sun runs its mandated course.*

B9,93,476 Mohammed: "There are five unseen keys known only to Allah: only Allah knows what will happen tomorrow; only Allah knows whether a child will be born as a male or a female; only Allah can predict the weather; only Allah knows when and where a person will die."

B8,74,246 Mohammed said, "Allah created Adam in the perfect human shape and size, nearly ninety feet tall. When Allah created Adam, he said, 'Go and introduce yourself to the angels sitting there. Pay attention to their greeting because that is the manner in which you and your descendents will greet others.' Adam went to the angels and said, 'As-Salamu Alaikum (Peace be upon you).' The angels responded, 'As Salamu-Alaika wa Rahmatullah (Peace and Allah's mercy be on you)."

Mohammed also said, "Everyone entering Paradise will do so in the perfect and original form and shape of Adam, rather than their present stature, which is continually diminishing."

B4,55,549 Mohammed said about human conception, for the first forty days after conception, each of us forms in a mother's womb. The next forty days is spent as a clot of blood, and the next forty as a bit of flesh. Then an angel is sent by Allah to write four determining words that signify a persons destiny: his actions, his time of death, his occupation, and whether he will be blessed or cursed by Allah. A soul is then infused in his body.

B4,55,546 Hearing of Mohammed's imminent arrival in Medina, Abdullah went to him and said, "I have three questions for you that only a prophet can answer: What is the first sign of the Hour of Reckoning? What will be the first meal served in Paradise? Why does a child look like his father, and why will it look like it's mother's brother?"

Mohammed said, "Gabriel has just given me those answers." Abdullah said, "Of all the angels, Gabriel is the greatest enemy of the Jews." Mohammed continued, "The first sign of the judgment is a great fire that unites the people of the east and the west; the people of Paradise will first dine on fish liver; if during intercourse the man climaxes first, the resulting child will look like him, if the woman climaxes first, then the child will look like her."

CURES

B4,54,483 In Mecca, I [Abu] often sat with Ibn Abbas. One time I had a fever and he told me, "Take Zam-zam water [a well in Mecca] to relieve a fever because Mohammed said a fever is caused by the heat from the fires of Hell; alleviate it with water, or Zam-zam water."

B7,67,446 Mohammed was asked about a mouse that fell into some butter fat and died. He said to dispose of the mouse and the butter-fat around it, but keep and eat the remaining butter fat."

B7,71,673 Mohammed: "If a fly drops into a container of liquid, submerge it in the liquid and throw the fly away. In one wing of the fly is a disease, but in the other is a cure for the disease."

B7,71,591 While traveling to Medina, Ghalib contracted an illness. Ibn Abi Atiq went to him and told us, "Treat the illness with black cumin. Grind five or seven seeds and add oil. Drop the mixture in both nostrils because Aisha related to me that she heard Mohammed say that black cumin can cure any disease except As-Sam. Aisha asked, 'What is As-Sam?' Mohammed replied, 'Death.'"

B7,71,592 I [Abu Huraira] was there when Mohammed said, "Black cumin can cure every disease except death."

B7,71,611 My son suffered from a disease of the throat and tonsils which I [Um Qais] had treated by pressing my fingers on his palate and tonsils. I took the boy with me to see Mohammed, and he asked me, "Why do press your son's throat and cause him pain? Treat him with Indian incense. It cures seven diseases, including pleurisy. To treat throat and tonsil disease, it is used as a snuff, and to treat pleurisy, it is placed in one side of the mouth."

Mohammed on disease.

B7,71,614 A man said to Mohammed, "My brother suffers from diarrhea." Mohammed said, "Tell him to drink honey." The man returned to Mohammed and said, "He drank the honey, but it made his condition worse." Mohammed said, "Allah tells the truth and your brother's stomach tells a lie."

This is the Sunna of Mohammed

ANIMALS

CHAPTER 15

8:46 Obey Allah and His messenger, and do not argue with
one another for fear that you will lose courage and strength.

DOGS

B1,4,173 Mohammed: "It is vital that a dish be washed seven times if a dog drinks from it."

B3,39,515 Mohammed: "One Qirat's worth of reward shall be deducted daily from a person's accumulated good deeds for owning a dog that doesn't hunt or guard a farm."

B7,67,389 Mohammed: "Anyone who keeps a dog as merely a pet, and not a hunting or guard dog, shall have two Qirats deducted every day from his accumulated good deeds."

B1,9,490 I [Aisha] was told of several things that can negate a prayer. I was told, "Prayer is nullified by a dog, an ass, or a woman that passes before people in prayer." I said, "You have turned women into dogs."

M004,1032 Mohammed said, "If any of you stand for prayer with an object as big as a saddle's rear in front of you, or if an ass, a woman, or a black dog passes in front of you, your prayer will be blocked." Someone asked, "Abu Dharr, what is it about a black dog that makes it different from a red or a yellow dog?" Abu Dharr said, "I asked the same thing of Mohammed, and he said, "A black dog is a devil.""

M010,3813 Mohammed gave an order to kill dogs, which we obeyed so faithfully that we even killed the dog that accompanied a woman coming from the desert. Mohammed later rescinded this order, but he did say, "It is your obligation to kill a black dog even if it has white spots over the eyes because it is a devil."

B3,34,439 Mohammed banned receiving money in exchange for a dog, in exchange for sex, or in exchange for fortune telling.

SNAKES

B4,54,518 I [Ibn Umar] witnessed Mohammed give a sermon. He said, "Kill snakes when you can. Take special care to kill any snake with two white lines down its back, or a snake with a stumpy or mutilated tail. They cause blindness and miscarriages."

B4,54,527 Mohammed: "Kill snakes with two white lines on their backs; they cause blindness and miscarriages."

B4,54,529 It was Ibn Umar's practice to kill snakes, but later he forbade the practice. He said, "One time Mohammed saw a snake skin that had been recently shed. He said, 'Find that snake and kill it.' It was because of this that I would kill snakes. I changed my practice when later Abu Lubaba told me that Mohammed had said, 'Do not kill all snakes, just those that have shortened or mutilated tails with two white lines down the back. Kill those snakes because they cause blindness and miscarriages.'"

OTHER ANIMALS

B4,55,579 Mohammed ordered that salamanders should be killed because, "They spit fire on Abraham."

B3,36,484 Mohammed banned the accepting of money for breeding fees.

B4,52,115 Mohammed allotted two shares of spoils of war to each horse and one share to each rider who participated in jihad.

B3,29,54 Mohammed: "It is not a sin for a pilgrim to slay certain animals: Crows, kites, mice, scorpions, and rabid dogs."

M020,4621 Mohammed: "Allah's blessings reside in the forelocks of war horses."

M035,6581 Mohammed: "If you hear a cock crowing, ask Allah for His good will because the cock sees angels. If you hear a donkey braying, ask Allah for His protection, because the donkey sees Satan."

This is the Sunna of Mohammed

ART

CHAPTER 16

*4:170 People! The Messenger has come to you with truth
from your Lord. If you believe, it will be better for you. But
if you do not believe, know that all that is in the heavens
and earth belongs to Allah. Allah is all-knowing ↝ ɪd wise!*

B7,72,843 Mohammed grew depressed one day after Gabriel's promised visit was delayed. When Gabriel came at last, Mohammed complained about the delay. Gabriel said to him, "Angels will not enter a house that contains a dog or a picture."

B8,73,130 There was once a curtain with pictures of animals on it in my [Aisha's] house. When Mohammed saw it, his face became flushed with anger. He tore it to bits and said, "People that paint such pictures will receive Hell's most terrible punishment on Judgment Day."

B4,54,447 One time I [Aisha] created a stuffed pillow for Mohammed and decorated it with pictures of animals. He came in with some other people one day, and I noticed a look of excitement on his face. I asked, "What is wrong?" He replied, "What is that pillow doing here?" I answered, "I made that for you so that you could lie on it." He said, "Are you not aware that angels will not enter a house with pictures in it and that the person that makes such pictures will be punished on Judgment Day until he gives life to that which he has made?"

B3,34,428 Ibn Abbas and I were together one day when a man came to him and said, "Ibn Abbas, I am a painter and my livelihood comes from these pictures." Ibn Abbas said, "I only know what Mohammed tells me, and I heard him say, 'Anyone who paints a portrait will continue to receive Allah's punishment until he can bring the picture to life, which of course, a man can not do.'"

The man turned pale and he breathed a heavy sigh upon hearing this. Ibn Abbas said, "That is a shame. If you must make pictures, then my advice is to make pictures of inanimate objects, like trees."

This is the Sunna of Mohammed

MOHAMMED

CHAPTER 17

*64:12 So obey Allah and His messenger. But if you turn
your backs to them, Our messenger is not to blame,
for his duty is only to deliver Our warning clearly.*

HIS PHYSICAL APPEARANCE

B7,72,791 Qatada asked Anas to describe Mohammed's hair. Anas said, "Mohammed's hair reached almost to his shoulders. It was wavy. Not straight, but not very curly, either.

B7,72,793 Mohammed had a unique look to him. He had big feet and hands, but his palms were soft.

B4,56,751 Mohammed was of average height and had wide shoulders and long hair. I saw him wearing a red cloak one time, and I thought he was the most handsome man I had ever seen.

MOHAMMED'S WHITENESS

There are many hadiths that report Mohammed's whiteness.

B4,56,765 When Mohammed prostrated himself to pray, he would spread his arms so wide apart, that we could see his armpits. Ibn Bukair described it as "the whiteness of his armpits."

B9,90,342 At the battle of Al-Ahzab, Mohammed helped us carry dirt to the fortifications. We could see the dust covering his white belly.

B1,3,63 We were sitting with Mohammed in the Mosque one day when a man rode up on a camel. He asked, "Which one of you is Mohammed?" We answered, "That white man leaning on his arm..."

HIS ANGER

There are many hadiths about Mohammed's anger.

B1,2,19 If Mohammed ordered a Muslim to do something, he made sure that it was something that was easily done, something within their limits of strength or endurance. Still, many complained, "Mohammed, we can't do that. We are not like you. Allah has freed you from all sin." The anger was apparent on Mohammed's face and he said, "No one fears Allah more than I, and I know Allah better than any of you."

B1,3,90 A man once said to Mohammed, "I may not be able to go to the obligatory prayer because our Imam is very long-winded when he leads the ceremony." The narrator continued, "I had never seen Mohammed more angry. He said, 'Some of you are making the others dislike praying. If you lead the prayers, then you should keep it brief. Some of the people are sick, weak, or simply have work to do.'"

HIS WIFE AISHA

Aisha was his favorite wife. This dream occurred when she was six.

M031,5977 Aisha quotes Mohammed: "Three nights in a row I saw you in a dream. An angel delivered you wrapped in silks and said, 'This is your wife.' As I unwrapped the silk, your face appeared. I said, 'If this dream is indeed from Allah, then let Him make it happen.'"

M008,3309 Mohammed and I [Aisha] were married when I was six. I was brought to his house when I was nine. We moved to Medina where I fell sick with a fever for a month. My hair fell out as a result of the illness. My mother, Umm Ruman, came for me one day as I was playing on a swing with some friends. I had no idea what she wanted, but she took me by the hand and had me stand by the door of our house. I was out of breath, but when I had composed myself, my mother took me inside and handed me over to some of the Helper women who proceeded to wish me good luck. The women washed me and made me pretty. Mohammed came in the morning and I was given to him.

M031,5981 Aisha relates that she and her friends often played with dolls while Mohammed was present, but when he came over, her friends would hide from him because of shyness. He would, however, call them back to play with her.

SEX

B1,5,249 Narrated by Maimuna, a wife of Mohammed: After sex, Mohammed purified himself just as he would for prayer except that he would not wash his feet. He would rinse off the semen and vaginal secretions from his penis and then pour water over the rest of his body. He would then remove his feet from the bathtub and wash them. That was how Mohammed cleaned himself after sex.

B7,71,660 Magic was used upon Mohammed that caused him to think that he had sex with his wives, when in fact he had not. One day he said to Aisha, "I have had a revelation from Allah about that problem that has been bothering me. Two men came to me in a dream; one of them sat by my head and the other at my feet. The first one asked the other, 'What is this man's problem?' The other replied, 'He is under a magic spell.' The first man asked, 'Who's spell is he under?' The other man answered, 'Labid, a hypocrite and an ally of the Jews.' The first man then asked the other, 'What was used to cast the spell?' 'A comb with Mohammed's hair in it,' he was told. 'Where is this comb?' the first man asked. 'In a bag made from a date palm. It is hidden under a rock in the Dharwan well,' the other man told him."

Mohammed went to Dharwan and removed the bag containing the comb. He said, "That was the well I saw in my dream. Its water was the color of Henna and the date palms surrounding it resembled the heads of devils. I took out the bag with the hexed comb in it." Aisha said to Mohammed, "Why didn't you take Nashra to treat your malady?" Mohammed said, "It was not necessary. Allah had already cured me. Besides, I don't want evil (magic) to establish itself among the people."

HABITS

B1,4,169 Mohammed would perform all tasks by working from right to left. This included putting on his shoes, combing his hair, or washing himself.

B1,6,298 Mohammed and I [Aisha] would bathe together after sex in the same tub. During my period, he would have me wear a dress that only covered me from the waist down and he would fondle me. He would also let me wash his head while I was menstruating.

B7,65,292 Mohammed preferred to begin things from the right side; combing his hair, putting on his shoes, or performing ablution. He would follow this practice in every thing he did.

M023,5018 Anas said that Mohammed forbade people to drink while standing. Qatada related: We asked him, "What about eating while standing?" Anas said, "That is even more objectionable."

M023,5029 Anas related the story that Mohammed would drink his refreshments in three gulps.

M023,5037 Mohammed: "When a Muslim eats, they should not wipe their hand until it is licked clean, either by themselves or by someone else."

M024,5234 Mohammed made it illegal for a man to eat with his left hand or walk with only one sandal on. He also forbade a man to wear a garment that had no opening for the arms to extend or support himself when wearing a single garment that might expose his genitalia.

M024,5238 Mohammed: "No one should lie on his back with one foot placed on top of the other."

Mohammed seems to have been exceptionally modest about his body.

B7,72,807 One day a man peeped into Mohammed's house and saw him scratching his head with a comb. Noticing the man Mohammed said, "If I had realized that you were peeking at me I would have stuck this comb in your eye. The reason that people must ask permission is to keep them from seeing things that they shouldn't."

MOHAMMED'S SLAVES

B3,34,351 A man committed himself to freeing one of his slaves upon his death, but later needed money. Mohammed took the slave and asked, "Does anyone want to buy this slave from me?" Nu Aim received the slave from Mohammed after giving the Prophet a certain price.

B7,65,344 While at the house of his slave tailor, Mohammed ate a gourd dish that he seemed to enjoy. Ever since then, I [Anas] have enjoyed eating gourd.

B9,91,368 Umar sought Mohammed and found him in an upstairs room with a black slave standing guard at the top of the stairs. Umar said to the slave, "Inform Mohammed that Umar is here and seeks permission to see him." The slave then admitted me to the room.

WAR

Mohammed was devoted to violence in the cause of Islam.

B9,90,332 Abu Huraira overheard Mohammed say, "By Allah, if I had a way of transporting all the men who wished to fight in jihad, I would not miss any opportunity to fight the Kafir. It would be a pleasure to be martyred for Allah, be resurrected, and martyred again and again."

Humor in jihad.

M031,5932 Amir B. Sa'd reported, on the authority of his father, that Allah's Apostle gathered his parents for him on the Day of Uhud when a polytheist had set fire to (i.e. attacked fiercely) the Muslims. Thereupon Allah's Apostle said to him: "(Sa'd), shoot an arrow, (Sa'd), may my mother and father be taken as ransom for you." I drew an arrow and I shot a featherless arrow at the Meccan polytheist, aiming his side. He fell down and his private parts were exposed. Allah's Messenger laughed so that I saw his front teeth.

CRUELTY

B2,24,577 Some people came to Medina, but the climate made them sick, so Mohammed gave them permission to stay among the camels that had been collected for taxes. He told them to drink the camel's urine and milk, as that would cure their illness. However, the people instead murdered the shepherd and stole the camels. Mohammed sent men after them and they were quickly captured. Mohammed ordered that their hands and feet be cut off, and their eyes pierced with hot pokers. They were left to die of thirst on the rocks of Harra.

HIS BODILY FUNCTIONS

One of many hadiths about Mohammed and elimination.

B1,9,479 Whenever Mohammed went to the toilet, another boy and I would follow with a stick, a staff and a container of water. When he finished, we would give him the water.

This is the Sunna of Mohammed

COMMENTS

CHAPTER 18

*9:63 Do they not know that whoever opposes Allah
and His Messenger will abide in the Fire of Hell, where
they will remain forever? This is the great shame.*

DUALITY

The Hadith divides humanity into two groups, Muslims and Kafirs. The Koran and the Sira present this same world view.

Each group has a different set of ethics so we call this dual ethics. There is one set that tells how to treat the Muslims and a second that describes how to treat the Kafir.

Non-Muslims can be treated kindly or they can be treated as the enemies of Allah. Their goods can be taken; they can be insulted, enslaved, and murdered if such treatment will advance Islam.

POLITICAL DUALITY

The Hadith contain the Sunna of jihad, slavery, dhimmis, and apostates. These are political issues with an ethical foundation. The suffering caused by jihad, slavery, dhimmis, and the killing of apostates is all based upon dualistic Islamic ethics. It is an absolute ethical inequality that is divine, sanctioned by the only god of the universe, Allah. This inequality between Muslim and Kafir is permanent and universal. It cannot be changed, reformed, or modified.

However, in either set of ethics, one point remains. A Kafir is never the equal of a Muslim. Islam may respect a Kafir but can never accept him as equal.

The Koran, Hadith, and Sira are emphatic. The only politics that can exist are the politics of Islam. Non-Muslims' politics are subject to the violence of jihad if the Kafirs do not submit. All governments must rule by Islamic Sharia law to achieve the peace of Islam.

UNITARY AND DUAL ETHICS

Unitary ethics are based upon the principle that at some fundamental level, all people are the same humanity, although they are not necessarily equal, as all people do not have the same abilities. This "sameness" means that we all want to be treated fairly. The perfect unitary ethical statement is: "Treat others as you wish to be treated." "Others" here means all of humanity is to be treated the same. This is an ideal perhaps, but failure to act upon it does not detract from its principle.

Dualistic Ethics

Give good advice to every Muslim.

A Muslim is a brother to every Muslim.

A Muslim is one who avoids harming any Muslim with his tongue or hands.

Unitary Ethics

Give good advice to every person.

A person is a brother/sister to every person.

A person avoids harming any person with his tongue or hands.

The dual ethics of Islam are not as simple as having separate ethics for the Kafir. What makes Political Islam so effective is that it has two stages of ethics for the Kafir, the ethics of the Meccan Koran and the ethics of the Medinan Koran. Islam can treat the Kafir well but as an inferior (Mecca) or treat him as an enemy of Allah (Medina). Both actions are sanctioned as sacred in the Koran. Muslims usually refer to the Meccan ethics when speaking to Kafirs. Apologists declare that the Meccan ethical system is the "real" Islam and that reform is possible.

Consider the comparisons between unitary and dualistic ethics in the table on the next page. These differences are not compatible. There is no middle ground or compromise between dualism and unitary ethics. They are mutually exclusive. Co-existence is temporary.

THE REAL ISLAM

What is the real Islam? Radical Islam? Fundamentalist Islam? Moderate Islam? Meccan Islam? Medinan Islam? There is only Islam. Islam is like a rainbow, a full-spectrum political system. Those who argue that the real Islam is moderate or that the real Islam is fundamentalist are like those who would say that a rainbow is red or green. A rainbow is not red, not green. No, a rainbow is all the colors. Islam is not peaceful, not violent. Islam is peaceful and violent. You can no more remove the aggression than you can remove the red from the rainbow. The only true view is to take the whole of Islam. The Islamic political doctrine always has two choices, and both choices are true. Political Islam is profoundly dualistic.

THE MECCAN IDEALS OF DUALISM	THE MEDINAN IDEALS OF DUALISM	THE IDEALS OF UNITARY ETHICS
Islam is the religion of peace. A real Muslim is never violent.	Violence and threats are used against Kafirs. The violence is caused by the Kafirs failure to submit to Islam.	Peace is the desired state between groups.
Artists and intellectuals are pressured.	Artists and intellectuals that offend Islam are threatened and/or killed. Art and ideas must submit to Islam.	Artists and intellectuals are free to speak.
Islam is the "brother" religion of the Jews and Christians.	All religions must submit to Islam.	All religions are tolerated.
Demands are made on the host culture to accommodate Islam.	Differences are settled by threats and force (any compromise is temporary).	Differences are settled by negotiation and compromise.
Local laws are obeyed outside the Islamic community.	Islamic law (Sharia) is supreme. Kafirs are second class subjects.	All people are equal before the law.
Islam's poverty is caused by the Kafirs.	Islam takes wealth as its due.	Wealth is generated and created.

This dualism cannot be removed. Dualism is at the core of the Trilogy. The Trilogy is perfect, permanent, and universal. It cannot be changed. A Muslim may reform but Islam cannot.

FOR MORE INFORMATION

www.politicalislam.com
www.cspii.org
Facebook: @BillWarnerAuthor
Twitter: @politicalislam
YouTube: Political Islam

CPSIA information can be obtained
at www.ICGtesting.com
Printed in the USA
LVOW07s1341280717

542134LV00003B/20/P